D0710768

ANTHOLOGY OF CONTEMPORARY
ITALIAN PROSE

ANTHOLOGY OF CONTEMPORARY ITALIAN PROSE

Compiled, Translated and Edited by
FRANCIS M. GUERCIO, B.A. (Hons.)

KENNIKAT PRESS
Port Washington, N. Y./London

ANTHOLOGY OF CONTEMPORARY ITALIAN PROSE

First published in 1931
Reissued in 1970 by Kennikat Press
Library of Congress Catalog Card No: 79-103226
SBN 8046-0863-6

Manufactured by Taylor Publishing Company   Dallas, Texas

CONTENTS

PREFACE

A RAPID, comprehensive survey of a literary phase, however limited its compass may be in space and time, can be at best only an approximation " by defect." The phenomena to be presented, classified and explained, are so complex and far-reaching in their ramifications, that the critic's wisest course is to limit himself to pointing out general lines of development, and to avoid specifications and subdivisions as much as possible, lest he should eventually discover that he has made for his subject, not an ideal mould, but a Procrustean bed.

This principle would appear to be particularly necessary in the treatment of twentieth-century Italian literature : a literary phase which may safely be ranked among the least homogeneous in the history of European letters.

Contemporary Italian literature shares with English, French, German and Spanish literature of the present day a number of general tendencies, some of which, as we shall show later on, were started by Italians or received in Italy their most vigorous support. But contemporary Italian literature, although partaking in the general movements of European literature, has a certain peculiar feature of its own, which goes to heighten its colour, variety and individuality, namely its regionalism.

The great number of clearly differentiated dialects still spoken in Italy could not fail to exert their influence upon a literature which, while it is characterised on the one hand by daring experimentation, is on the other continually endeavouring to introduce dialectisms or colloquialisms in order to convey as directly and spontaneously as possible the actual feelings and thoughts of mankind.

All Italian dialects, from Piedmontese to Sicilian, and not Tuscan only, as with the *puristi* of the eighteenth and nineteenth centuries, have been allowed to overflow into contemporary literature, with the result that the greatest writers do not disdain to use local phrases and expressions, either in their original form or slightly modified to suit the requirements of literature. But more significant still than the regionalism or particularism of diction are the accompanying psychological differences and contrasts which characterise Italian authors according to the part of the country they come from to an extent unknown in England, and only feebly paralleled in France, Germany and Spain.

Thus a distinct group is constituted by the writers of Lombardy and Piedmont, the heirs of Manzoni and partly of Ippolito Nievo, but more immediately of C. Dossi and G. P. Lucini, aristocratic and distinctive in their traits, full of reserve, also characterised by a tendency to moralise and by an interest in political and social problems, a group represented on the one hand by C. Linati and the contributors to the *Convegno* and on the other by G. Cena, V. Brocchi, S. Gotta and G. Bertacchi.

Another group is formed by the Tuscans, distinguished at once by their humanistic refinement and their plebeian vigour, excelling in the widely different realms of polemics, of broad historical reconstruction and of the evocation of every-day existence. These writers are the immediate followers and successors of Carducci, Fucini and F. Martini, and include G. Papini, A. Soffici, E. Cecchi, B. Cicognani, L. Viani, C. Malaparte and others.

The literature of Romagna, another distinct regional group in Italian literature as a whole, is more difficult to characterise psychologically, because it would appear to alternate between two opposite and divergent tempers : the ardent, tumultuous, vehemently destructive and creative spirit of men like A. Oriani and B. Mussolini, and the tender, idyllic spirit of Pascoli, S. Ferrari and M. Moretti. These opposite tempers are in reality but different aspects of a nature that concentrates on the contemplation and education of intuitive values, whether in life or in art, and confers upon the thinker an almost prophetic character and upon all prose something of the rhapsody of poetry. The literature of Romagna is distinguished from that of Lombardy and Piedmont by its lack of practical sense, and from the Tuscan literature by its freedom from preciosity and plebeianism and a certain absence of plastic form : it is essentially meditative and introvertive, and its exquisite perception of external things is prompted by and correlated with inner moods. A. Panzini, A. Beltramelli and R. Serra are further representatives of this group.

A fourth group is constituted by the Neapolitan poets, novelists and philosophers. Here we find the naïve and picturesque sentimentality of the popular songs and ballads of Naples embodied in the works of S. Di Giacomo, C. Russo and M. Serao, and at the same time a vein of acute philosophical criticism which, although universal in its appeal, shows in its caustic wit certain local traits, as in the less technical works of B. Croce.

A fifth group comprises the island writers, viz. the Sicilians G. Verga, L. Capuana, G. A. Borgese, L. Pirandello, the Neapolitan F. de Roberto, who may be regarded as a follower of Verga, and the Sardinian G. Deledda. In these there is, on the one hand, the greatest intensity of passion and fertility of imagination exemplified in the representation of actual or fictitious life, as in Verga and Capuana, and on the other, a cool, relentless analysis of human nature pursued to the threshold and sometimes to the inclusion of the deepest philosophical problems, as in the plays and novels of L. Pirandello.

Among the many minor regional groups there is the singular Triestin contingent, comprising S. Slataper, C. Michelstaedter, U. Saba and I. Svevo. These writers have in common a tendency towards a mysticism and introspection which is not entirely germane to the Italian character. There is a touch of morbidity and melancholia in them which can perhaps be best explained by their Slavonic racial connections and their more direct contact with the thought and culture of Central and Eastern Europe.

The above are the regional groupings which would appear with the greatest prominence in a general panorama of contemporary Italian literature. The names of many authors in each group have been omitted, partly in order to avoid overcrowding the canvas, and thereby obscuring the view, and partly in order to give greater prominence to the leading lights.

This regionalism, which has enriched and varied so magnificently not only the Italian literature of to-day but the Italian literature of every age, from Dante's to our own, carries with it the inseparable danger of disgregation, *i.e.* the danger of a particularism that might lose sight of the fundamental linguistic and cultural unity of the Italian people.

Hence a unitary, nationalistic bias in a certain number of Italian authors of all ages, a bias which in our time has been stressed by G. D'Annunzio and A. Oriani. The former's most popular works in Italy have long been those in which he has magnified the greatness of the Italian race, prophesying or invoking a return of its ancient prestige and power (*La nave* and the *Laudi*), while the latter, a powerful thinker and historian, has developed the nationalist thesis of the revival of Latin civilisation centred in Rome and has been in the realm of political thought one of the forerunners of Fascism. Parallel ideas and tendencies are traceable in Marinetti, the founder of Futurism, and here and there in nearly all the writers of the *Voce* group.

More exclusively literary is the neo-classical reaction in favour of a genuinely Italian style of writing modelled upon the great classics of the past, and more especially upon Leopardi. This reaction, which has strengthened considerably since the War, is directed on the one hand against any kind of particularism in language or style and on the other against a number of modern literary experiments which may be broadly characterised as futuristic, and which have been carried out or upheld by a large number of contemporary authors. C. Linati, E. Cecchi, V. Cardarelli, R. Bacchelli and A. Soffici, in his latest phase, are supporters of this reaction.

But Italian literary regionalism, and the unitary movements which oppose or check it, should not obscure the view of the more fundamental and universal aspects of contemporary Italian literature, which not only override all regional distinctions, but connect Italy indissolubly with the general trend of ideas in Europe and in the Western World. These broader tendencies are especially apparent in the more significant literary works, aiming primarily at the development of ideas, and resolve themselves, fundamentally, into a reaction against the materialism and positivism of the second half of the nineteenth century. This reaction is sometimes spontaneous, purely intuitive, as in the case of Panzini, but more often, and in fact more frequently than in any other country, essentially philosophical, *i.e.* consciously and reflectively elaborated. Papini and Soffici are probably the authors in whom this revulsion to free, subjective values is most clearly marked. Papini's *Tragico quotidiano, Il crepuscolo dei filosofi, Il pilota cieco, Un uomo finito,* and Soffici's *Scoperte e massacri, Statue e fantocci,* and to a certain extent the *Giornale di bordo,* are more in the nature of vividly coloured philosophical autobiographies and diaries than of purely literary composition.

Others in whom this ardent preoccupation with philosophical issues is apparent, although in a lesser degree, are G. Prezzolini, G. Amendola, S. Slataper, P. Jahier, R. Serra, and E. Cecchi. Nor can we forget here, relatively ephemeral though it may be, the *futurist* movement, founded by Marinetti in 1909, which has had considerable influence abroad in the domain of plastic art, and which from 1913 to 1915 was supported by Papini and Soffici in their review *Lacerba.*

The general idealistic reaction, led by the above-mentioned contributors to the *Voce,* manifesting itself under the various guises of " individualism," " impressionism," " intuitivism," " futurism," " relativism," etc., is intimately bound up with the contemporary developments of Italian and European philosophical thought.

Nor is Italy alone in this literary reaction to a philosophical stimulus. French symbolism and

German expressionism are similar responses in the domain of literature to idealistic, intuitionist movements in philosophy. But it is especially to the powerful influence of Benedetto Croce and Giovanni Gentile that we must look, if we would discover the immediate source of the prevailing temper of contemporary Italian literature.

Croce's *Estetica*, his *Letteratura della nuova Italia* and his innumerable articles of a doctrinal and polemical character published in the *Critica*, Gentile's *Teoria dello Spirito come atto puro* and his frequent dissertations and lectures on Italian philosophy and literature, may be regarded as having exercised on the Italian literary world an influence rarely, if ever, paralleled by any philosophers in the realm of letters. This influence is due mainly to the prominence given by Croce in his philosophy to the question of art, and more particularly to the sense of freedom from mechanism which he has been able to restore to it, after the oppressive determinism of the positivist or materialistic outlook. In Croce's *Weltanshaung*, the writer and the artist, generally, feel themselves restored to their long-lost position of autonomous creators of values.

But Croce's powerful dialectic would not have been sufficient of itself to gain for him the enthusiastic interest of men of letters. His rich and many-sided personality and his admirably lucid style have contributed largely towards the full realisation of what might have remained a cold intellectual assent.

Besides Croce and Gentile, other thinkers have been influential in directing the present-day tendencies of Italian literature. Through the *Voce*, founded in 1909, the influence of Bergson's intuitionism has been felt, and notably in Ardengo Soffici.

Another European thinker who has exercised a considerable influence over Italian literature during the last three or four decades is F. Nietzsche. His concept of the " superman," variously presented and elaborated, has played a most important part in D'Annunzio's more mature works (*Laus vitae*, *Più che l'amore*, *Forse che sì*, *forse che no*, etc.), and his influence over the younger writers appears clearly in Papini, in Soffici and in the post-War writer, Attilio della Torre.

A singular literary work, inspired or at least profoundly affected by Freud's theories of the subconscious, is Italo Svevo's *La coscienza di Zeno*.

Curiously concurrent in many respects with modern psycho-analytical speculations, and yet absolutely independent in its origin, is the art of L. Pirandello, from a European point of view perhaps the best-known manifestation of contemporary Italian literature. Originally a writer of racy Sicilian stories, Pirandello has recently developed into an author of dramas and novels in which some of the problems that torment the modern Western mind are presented in the most adequate and forcible manner. The problems

with which Pirandello deals are often of a Freud-
ian nature, and this has certainly added to the
interest in his plays and novels in many quarters ;
but his sphere is wider than that of the mere
subconscious: his theme is the difficulties and
perplexities, sometimes lightly humorous and
at other times intensely tragic, which arise from
the conflict between life in its Protean flux and
the forms into which men desire or find it necessary to constrain it. Pirandello's treatment of
this conflict is essentially psychological, for it is the
drama that takes place in the mind that concerns
him ; consequently his comedies and tragedies
relate to psychological realisations or discoveries,
and not to outward events.

The novelty of Pirandello's works does not,
however, consist in their being psychological,
but in the nature of the psychological problems
raised. It consists in the effectiveness with
which abstruse and seemingly abnormal psychological entanglements are unravelled in the
course of a story or play possessing undeniable
verisimilitude. This characteristic confers upon
Pirandello's works an eminently speculative tone,
which does not on the other hand diminish their
value as artistic creations. What is indeed
singular is the forcible, convincing manner in
which contemporary Italian authors have succeeded in presenting, whether in autobiography,
or by means of the novel and the short story, or on
the stage, the deepest and most universal queries
of contemporary philosophy and psychology.

Passing from our general view of contemporary Italian literature to the individual author, we must state at once that within the narrow compass of a short preface there will be room only for general remarks on the particular authors of which samples are given in the following anthology.

The general features of Pirandello's work have already been outlined. His European fame is connected with his dramatic works, his novels and short stories being little known outside Italy. His short stories, of which two are given in this anthology, are remarkable for their simplicity of plot and clarity of narrative. The realistic foundation upon which all Pirandello's subsequent art has been raised is clearly apparent in these stories, over four hundred in number, in which Italian middle-class and peasant life is portrayed with a vividness and objective veracity worthy of Pirandello's fellow-countryman G. Verga. But the central theme of Pirandello's stories is not, as with Verga, the vicissitudes of tragic passion or pathos, but the humorous or perplexing contradictions and the mutual incomprehensibilities of men's natures. He generally introduces characters whose points of view are hopelessly incompatible, beings who are inextricably wrapped up in their own passion and become thereby the laughing stock of others, persons who misjudge one another with ludicrous or tragic consequences ; or he throws into relief the mutability of man's spirit as shown in discontinuities and incoherences in the same man.

Widely different in character is Alfredo Panzini, probably the greatest novelist, in the more precise meaning of the term, of contemporary Italy. As opposed to the essential modernism of Pirandello, free alike from classical or historical reminiscences, Panzini's spirit is profoundly saturated with humanistic culture. An expounder of history and of the ancient classics by profession, Panzini's power and charm lie to a great extent in the happy introduction of historical parallels and contrasts, in a faculty for showing the reader how wonderfully different and yet essentially similar life in the different historical periods has been.

Panzini's novels all deal with contemporary life in Italy, and it must not be supposed that his profound professorial culture hinders or chills the concise modernity of his style, which is singularly clear and airy, not to say playful, though he never indulges in futuristic licence. His outlook on men and things is benevolently ironical, and rather distrustful of modern science and industrial progress. There is in Panzini a love for the country and for all things simple and humble which vividly recalls Pascoli, and essentially Pascolian is the tenderness and delicacy of his feeling when he is moved by love or pity.

A sharp contrast to the gentle irony of Panzini is the volcanic impetuosity of Giovanni Papini. We have already noted that a number of Papini's works, and indeed the more significant ones, are essentially philosophical autobiographies or diaries.   He is not, strictly speaking, a novelist.

Papini's outlook has suffered frequent and radical changes, and at every turn he has thrown himself into some new *credo* with all the ardent extremism of his nature.   He has been, in succession, a positivist, an idealist, a pragmatist, a futurist ; and now he professes conversion to Roman Catholicism.   His attitude is character-ised by an absolute sincerity and a fearless analysis of himself and of others, resulting in a stimulating although virulent criticism of modern life and thought.   His style is trenchant and spasmodic, issuing in brief, explosive sentences.   His diction is definitely Tuscan, and more tinged with local colour than that of either Pirandello or Panzini.

Ardengo Soffici is an outstanding representa-tive of purely æsthetic writing, supported by a keen interest in the more philosophical aspects of art criticism.   Essentially plastic in his imagina-tion, he revels in descriptions of nature, distin-guished by a great care and consideration for detail and a clearly defined colouring.   Soffici excels as a fragmentarist, and his finest works are more in the nature of collections of vignettes than of novels.   The critical vein in Soffici, to which we have already referred, is concerned mainly with art, and he has been one of the leaders of futurism in Italy (*Lacerba*), while his appreciations of contemporary French painting are of universal and lasting value (1).

1. See biographical note in the following anthology.

Another notable fragmentarist is Ugo Ojetti. Like Soffici, he is a distinguished art critic, but his interests are not exclusively æsthetic. All things appeal to his many-sided appreciation : buildings, pictures, landscapes, historical reminiscences, and above all human personalities, whose essential nature he knows how to depict with a few deft strokes. Perhaps no other contemporary writer has travelled so extensively or come into personal contact with so many of the famous men of our time as Ojetti. His volumes of reminiscences (*Cose viste*) constitute a vast survey, in impressionist sketches, of the main movements and personalities of the age, together with descriptions and anecdotes which are among the most perfect specimens of contemporary Italian prose.

Emilio Cecchi also deserves an honourable place among contemporary critics. His outlook is imbued with the æsthetic doctrines of Croce, and his originality consists in the successful combination of searching criticism with an exquisitely lyrical style. He excels in the characterisation of a writer or of a plastic artist by means of similes and metaphors, in entering into their spirit intuitively, thus rendering his criticism more a psychological re-creation than an *a posteriori* reflection.

Of the Italian writers of the Great War, we have thought good to include R. Serra and P. Jahier.

Renato Serra showed abundant promise of

becoming one of the leading literary critics of his time. His critical essays, although immature and often unconvincing, evince great acumen and a marvellous command of the Italian language. It is, however, his estimate of the ultimate effects of war upon literature and men of letters and, indirectly, upon mankind as a whole, that has earned for him his lasting reputation.

Piero Jahier is at once a War writer and a representative of that regional tendency which we have shown to be so strong in Italian literature. His theme is the life of the mountain peasants of Northern Italy, and more especially of the Waldensian communities which inhabit the valleys of the Pellice and of the Chisone. Before the War he had depicted their normal existence in an autobiographical study (*Ragazzo*) and during the War he showed the same men under arms, in the Alpine corps. His outlook is distinctly coloured with Protestant austerity and gloom, but in his War books it is mainly his patriotic and democratic sympathies that come to the fore. His style, while thoroughly imbued with the phraseology of his particular Piedmontese dialect, is at once intensely personal and fundamentally lyrical. He abounds in original constructions and juxtapositions, often in defiance of clarity and grammatical correctness ; and his prose often acquires the cadence and rhythm of poetry.

Ada Negri has only recently developed into a writer of Italian prose. She has been and she remains essentially a lyrist, full of ardent and tender sensibility. The intellectualism of Pirandello, the æstheticism of Soffici and the irony and pity of Panzini are alike removed from her more simple nature.

Massimo Bontempelli is something of an Italian David Garnett. His domain is the unreal, depicted with the faithful attention to detail normally associated with the real. Yet his fantastic stories are not mere excursions into the realm of the impossible : they generally throw into relief some psychological complex. His art makes little or no appeal to the emotions ; its success depends upon startling, novel conceptions, which upset the accepted order of existence or develop its potentialities to a chimerical degree.

Riccardo Bacchelli has already been mentioned as one of the supporters of the neo-classical reaction which upholds a genuinely Italian style of writing, in opposition to all literary experiments broadly qualifiable as futurist. Bacchelli excels as a novelist and as a writer of short stories. He is equally successful in the historical novel, in the fantastic fable or apologue and in the vivid description of Nature and everyday life. In all these different *genres* he is distinguished by an extraordinarily acute psychological insight and by a vein of good-humoured satire, but he is essentially a literary artist and his interest in facts and ideas never becomes so engrossing as to disturb the serenity of his art. His style is clear and agile, full of racy expressiveness, but free from particularist affectations.

Manfredo Vanni, although far less known than the aforesaid authors and definitely outside the sphere of what we may call " militant " contemporary literature, deserves an honourable place among contemporary story tellers and epigrammatists. His productions cannot rank in originality and significance with those of the better known writers, but in many of his short stories, which are modern counterparts to the old Italian *novelle* of the Middle Ages, the pure comedy of situation is handled with exquisite tact and a rare command of the resources of the Italian language. His epigrams are an acute, sparkling commentary, in the purest Tuscan vein, on contemporary life and manners.

In omitting to include extracts from more than a dozen other contemporary Italian authors of outstanding merit, the translator and compiler is conscious of having fallen short of completeness in his collection of samples of contemporary Italian prose. But in order to attain completeness, it would have been necessary to exceed the bounds of a short anthology. A selection has been made, therefore, which purports to include extracts from the greatest prose writers of present-day Italy, and extracts from those among the others whose works have been regarded as most suitable for translation.

On the score of unsuitability, all writings in

pure dialect have been discarded, and, unless unavoidable, all writings which would have to be amputated from the body of longer works.

The only case in which the compiler has had to resort to the latter expedient is in Serra's *Esame di coscienza* (Examination of Conscience), the only work from which it would be fair to take a representative extract, and one which unfortunately is continuous from beginning to end, with no divisions into chapters. In other cases, as in the selections from Papini's *Un uomo finito* (A Worn-out Man), in the extract from Jahier's *Con me e cogli alpini* (With me and with the Alpine Corps) or in the vignettes from Soffici's *Giornale di bordo* (Log-book), the passages selected are so self-contained and independent of their respective contexts that their abstraction from them can hardly be qualified as amputation. In all other cases, short stories, essays or fragments which are entirely self-contained have been chosen.

It may be advisable to explain briefly why D'Annunzio has not been given a place in this anthology. The first reason is that nearly all D'Annunzio's important prose works have already been published in English translations. The second reason is that D'Annunzio belongs definitely to the Italy of yesterday, at least in the greater number of his prose writings ; whereas the authors from whom selections are here given are representative of the Italy of to-day. Indeed one might go even further, and say that this

anthology includes at least two authors, Bontempelli and Bacchelli, in relation to whom
D'Annunzio belongs not to yesterday, but to the
day before yesterday. We must in fact recognise
that Bontempelli and Bacchelli, as also Fracchia,
Angioletti, Gadda and the other young writers
who have been winning laurels for themselves
during the last few years, represent a new gener-
ation in contemporary Italian literature which is
beginning to oust the older contemporaries.

The translations purport to be neither literal
nor free. The translator has endeavoured to be
as literal in his rendering as is compatible with
a thoroughly English diction and a perfect
clarity in conveying the *nuances* of the original.
Thus it has often been necessary to expand the
Italian text in order to make it clear in English,
and sometimes it has been found advisable in the
interests of literary *tournure* to condense the original, where a fewer number of English words
could express perfectly its meaning.

The translator would like to thank here those
friends who have very kindly assisted him in the
countless perplexities which have arisen during
the labour of translation, and more especially
Prof. P. Rebora of Manchester University, who
has made clear to him the meaning of many
obscure passages in the extracts from Serra and
Jahier.

Thanks are also due to the Italian authors and
publishers who have so courteously granted
permission to give extracts from works whose

copyrights were in their gift ; and to the editors
of *The Bermondsey Book* and of the *London
Mercury*, who have obligingly permitted the
reprint of the translations first published in these
periodicals (1).

F. GUERCIO.

MANCHESTER,
  November, 1930.

1. *N.B.*—In several cases, as for instance in the two *novelle*
by Pirandello, the edition quoted is the most recent, but not the
one actually used by the translator.

PIRANDELLO

Luigi Pirandello was born at Girgenti, in Sicily, in 1867. His higher studies were accomplished at Rome and at the university of Bonn, in Germany, where he submitted a thesis on Roman dialectology. On his return to Italy, he published a translation of Goethe's Roman elegies. From 1897 to 1921 he was professor of Italian literature at the *Istituto Superiore di Magistero* at Rome.

Up to forty-five years of age he had written only short stories and novels. He then began to write plays, and since the War his reputation as a playwright has become world-wide.

His principal works are : a number of short stories, written between 1894 and 1919, which are being collected together and published by R. Bemporad under the title of *Novelle per un anno* ; the following novels : *L'esclusa* (1901), *Il turno* (1902), *Il fu Mattia Pascal* (1904), *Suo marito* (1911), *I vecchi e i giovani* (1913), *Si gira* (1916), *Uno, nessuno e centomila* (1926) ; and the following plays, all written between 1912 and 1925, which are thus distributed in the first twenty volumes of the new republication of all Pirandello's dramatic works by R. Bemporad (Florence) : vol. 1, *Tutto per bene* ; vol. 2, *Come prima, meglio di prima* ; vol. 3, *Sei personaggi in cerca d'autore* ; vol. 4, *Enrico IV* ; vol. 5, *L'uomo, la bestia e la virtù* ; vol. 6, *La signora Morli, una e due* ; vol. 7, *Vestire gli ignudi* ;

vol. 8, *La vita che ti diedi* ; vol. 9, *Ciascuno a suo modo* ; vol. 10, *Così è (se vi pare)* ; vol. 11, *Pensaci, Giacomino !* ; vol. 12, *La sagra del Signore della nave, L'altro figlio, La giara* ; vol. 13, *Il piacere dell' onestà* ; vol. 14, *Il berretto a sonagli* ; vol. 15, *Il giuoco delle parti* ; vol. 16, *Ma non è una cosa seria* ; vol. 17, *L'innesto* ; vol. 18, *La ragione degli altri* ; vol. 19, *L'imbecille, Lumìe di Sicilia, Cecè, La patente* ; vol. 20, *All' uscita, Il dovere del medico, La morsa, L'uomo dal fiore in bocca.* His most recent plays are : *Diana e la Tuda* (1926), *L'amica delle mogli* (1927), *La nuova colonia* (1928), and *Lazzaro* (1929).

THE BLESSING

" I CAN'T make people out ! "—Don Marchino used to repeat at least twenty times a day, shrugging his shoulders, opening out his hands fanwise before his chest and turning down the corners of his mouth—" I can't make people out ! "

Because, in many and many cases, people did not behave as he would have behaved, or even because people very often took exception to what he did and to what seemed to him well done.

But—good heavens ! for what earthly reason had his Stravignano parishioners regarded him askance, from the very beginning ? They could not forgive his having turned into a farm (with the approval of his superiors, of course !) the oak grove that used to be behind the downstream chapel and that used to eat up all the parish living.

No, they hadn't been able to swallow that blessed farm yet, nor the small apartment of four rooms which he had caused to be built with the proceeds from the sale of the trees. That apartment was attached to the chapel, as was also a little landed house for himself and his sister Marianna. But hadn't a portion of that money been spent on restoring the chapel? and what harm was there in letting that apartment every year, during the summer time, to some family that came to rusticate at Stravignano?

The Stravignanese *would* have their parson poorer than Holy Job. And the beauty of it was this : that, on the one hand, he had to be everybody's servant, but woe to him, on the other hand, if he were seen spade in hand or attending to his animals. Because he shouldn't dirty his cassock, eh? Because the hands that touch the Consecrated Host should not become horny? Why, it was his conscience, his conscience, not his hands that ought not to be soiled or hardened !

Don Marchino was right, but, if indeed he ever looked at his person, he was no longer aware that both his sister and himself had, as it were, goose's legs, on which they waddled along just like two geese, of the same stature, fattish and neckless. Don Marchino didn't hear himself speaking, or even if he did he did not gather that his voice, weighed down by a perpetually obstructed nose, was like the miaouing of a cat.

Now his parishioners' antipathy was partly, and in no small degree, traceable to these things which he could not realise : his figure, his voice and also his peculiar way of speaking.

When, for instance, they went and asked him to lend his she-ass in a case of urgency, such as the necessity of a night call on the doctor at Nocera, Don Marchino would invariably answer :

" She won't let you get there. It would be a case of breaking your neck two or three times, my fine fellow ; I will only say three times, and leave it at that ! "

That is how he used to talk, often repeating such witty little phrases, which he had heard goodness knows where and from whom. But he had now come to repeat them as though they were a natural way of speaking, without any intention of being witty. Besides, that she-ass was really vicious, so much so that Don Marchino did not conscientiously believe he could risk the loan of her light-heartedly. Why, good heavens ! how many times she hadn't allowed him, even *him*, to get into the shandry ! (1). And in order to avoid being bitten or kicked, while he was saddling her or putting her in the shafts, he had to show the greatest politeness and utter many many sweet little words and paternally admonish her to be patient and resigned, since

1. Pirandello's *biroccio* and *biroccino* correspond more closely to *shandry* (a term widely used in Lancashire, Cheshire and North-Western England, generally) than to *cart*, *trap* or *float*. A *shandry* is a light, two-wheeled cart.

it had pleased God to bring her into this world as a she-ass.

" Why, naturally ! "—rejoined the Stravignanese. That she-ass, nearly always tended by Don Marchino, the hens and the three pigs, who were perpetually minded by sister Marianna, and the cows, in the care of Rosa, the barefooted maid, seeing that master with his sister going in and out among them like two geese, they were obliged to feel a certain animal affinity to them. This felt affinity made them take liberties which they certainly wouldn't have dared to take with other masters. And all laughed at the little respect which those ill-bred animals showed for their parson and his sister : at the teasing, perhaps amorous, which the three big scaly pigs inflicted on Marianna : at the latter's desperation when looking for the eggs, which the hens would purposely hide by running away into odd corners to lay. Those hens all had rings on their feet, that there might not be any mistake about them !

" And why not tie some pretty blue ribbons on the sucking-pigs' tails, *sǫra* (1) Marianna ? "

Now, see ! . . . Were these things one ought to say to the poor sister of a poor parson, who didn't even make himself a nuisance ' to the air ' ? Yet . . . and Don Marchino shrugged his shoulders, opened out his hands fanwise before his chest and, contracting the corners of his mouth, repeated : " I can't make people out ! "

1. A common abbreviation of *signora*.

He had more than ever good reason to repeat this wonted exclamation of his the day he went down to the cattle-market at Nocera.

He had nothing to buy and nothing to sell : he merely went to see and to hear. That year his contract with the parish farmers, with whom he was dissatisfied, expired, and he had already made known that the following year he would arrange with others. Now the time had come, and there at the fair he wanted to know who was buying and who was selling, and what was being said about one thing and another among the country folk gathered together from the whole neighbourhood. Those very people who were never seen in church, no, not even at the chief festivals, accused him of having that day left his parish in order to go mouching round at the fair until sunset.

But this was nothing. When he had already got into the shandry to return to Stravignano in that nasty wind which had so suddenly arisen, a certain Nunziata came up to him, with a boy about eight years old in her arms and a little goat behind her, calling upon him to help her for the love of God.

This Nunziata had as a little girl, many and many years ago, been in the service of the parish. Under Don Marchino's eyes she had become the most beautiful girl in Stravignano, and Don Marchino would have liked to give her in marriage to the son of his old farmer at that time, a good sort of a fellow, who had fallen in love with her. But all of a sudden, without caring to say why, she had turned her back on this youth and had married someone belonging to the neighbouring village of Sorìfa. Nine years had already elapsed ; Don Marchino had changed his farmer four times, and he was about to do so for the fifth time, and had not thought any more of Nunziata, who had left his parish. At Stravignano, it was said, at first, that she was doing well at Sorìfa, that her husband was a good worker; then, later, people began to say that things were not well with her, because her husband had been taken ill with an ugly kidney disease, which he had contracted through falling from a branch that had given way beneath him while he was pruning. It seemed that this malady had been brewing inwardly and had subsequently come out in leg swellings. Whereupon the doctor had forbidden him to work, advising him to remain in bed, well cared for and on a purely milk diet. Fine advice to give to one who lived by the use of his arms !

Don Marchino could hardly recognise her there, at Nocera, beggarly, barefooted and in that little frock, which was only the more piteous because it was trying to look new. But, what with the furious wind and the welter of men and animals hurrying back under the threat of a great storm, the she-ass had grown more fretful than ever and would not be controlled ; so upon Nunziata's asking him, for heaven's sake, to take that boy, who could no longer stand on his

feet and was ill, yes, worse than his father, in
the shandry as far as Stravignano, where she
would pick him up, later, on her way back to
Sorìfa along the main-road, Don Marchino,
who was making Herculean efforts to hold the
ass, felt provoked to the verge of ferocity and,
opening wide his eyes, cried : " But can't you
see, my daughter ! "

His vexation increased when some inquisitive
passers-by, who had stopped to gaze, thought
good to keep the ass still and quiet so that he
might listen at ease to what that poor woman,
so dejected, wanted of him ; and then, when he
persisted in refusing on the excuse of the peevish
moodiness of the ass, they cried that, by God,
he, a priest, ought to be ashamed to do so ! The
she-ass ? Why, what was that ! There, give
her a couple of lashes ! a couple of good hard
wrenches at the bridle ! That poor woman . . .
that poor little boy . . . why, look at him, as
yellow as wax ! and that nanny-goat. . . . Oh,
God, what was the matter with her ? you could
count her bones. . . . Ah, from Sorìfa ? had
the woman brought her down on foot from Sorìfa
to try and sell her ? how much ? nine crowns ?
ah, she had bought her for nine crowns ! . . .
now, not even half a crown. . . .

Wasn't it just the occasion for Don Marchino
to exclaim : " I can't make people out " ?

Under what obligation could he be, seeing
that that woman had not, for many years, belonged
to his parish ? for charity's sake ? imposed upon

him, like that? why, no, no and no again!
because it was, moreover, against all reason.
Charity be sugared! she, a mother, ought to
have been the first to be charitable, charitable
towards her child, by not bringing him such a
long way when he was ill; and it would have
been an easy charity. No, sir! to force into a
difficult deed of charity one who had no obligation thereto! difficult, certainly, difficult for
so many reasons! a load of that sort, a sick boy,
who couldn't sit upright, on an ass . . . why
yes! yes! it was for him to say, for him who
knew her well! on a she-ass that wouldn't hear
of further burdens, especially going up hill and
in all that wind. No, no, away! away! room
. . . room . . . and, threatening with his
switch, Don Marchino broke into a gallop,
followed by howls, whistles and other uncouth
noises.

The wind attacked him from behind, and
seemed bent on lifting him up off the steep
highway, donkey, shandry and all, just as it
raised the dust and the dry leaves.

When, at the close of evening, he climbed
down from the shandry in front of the chapel
adjoining the presbytery, there, at a bend in
the main road, he felt his arm aching with the
effort to hold on his best plush biretta, that
wanted to run away with that nasty, cursed wind,
which was howling so hard and making the
trees here in the avenue and there on the slope,
opposite the chapel, rustle so loudly that, see!

. . . Marianna hadn't heard the jingling of the ass's bell and had not promptly come, as usual, to give him a hand. He had to call for her, besides knocking on the door with the haft of his switch, at the risk—and how else ?—at the risk of damaging both switch and door.

Marianna, at the knocking, came out with a lamp. Well done, goose ! the wind put it out at once and . . . ugh, her petticoats ! why, goodness gracious, what a brain ! and the lamp ? all her petticoats turned up in front of her face and she, lamp in hand, 'asking' for a blaze. . . . Away, get inside ! get inside ! and Don Marchino, as cross as two sticks, set to work, alone, to unharness the ass, muttering, with reference also to his sister : " I can't make people out ! " . . .

Having led Nina to the stable, which had been hollowed out in the slope opposite the chapel, and having drawn the shandry in under cover, he said to his sister, before entering the presbytery, that it would be advisable to put out the tubs and washing-basins, because that night there would be rain without a doubt, rain that would bring the wind down. At Nocera he had heard the grumbling of thunder.

" It's still far away, but it's coming nearer. And to-night we shall get it right enough."

A little later, at supper, listlessly swallowing that thin broth which Rosa had prepared for him, he recounted to Marianna the venture he had come by at Nocera, dwelling on the fine brazenness of that Nunziata and the way they wanted to impose on him. But afterwards, comforted by the good, mild wine of his vineyard, which he used to sip with gusto for a good while after supper, he thought no more of it. He started talking about what he had seen and heard at the fair and, meanwhile, his hunger appeased and his heart content, he looked around that warm and comfortable little dining room, smoking his pipe, while Marianna was dressing Rosa's feet— out of charity, yes—but also that she might find no excuse next morning, at the break of dawn, for not taking the cows out to pasture.

The wind, outside, continued to howl more threateningly than ever.

The wind ? but no. Indeed it *was* someone knocking at the door.

" At this hour ? " said Don Marchino, looking in consternation at his sister and at the maid.

The latter went to see who it was, and brother and sister strained their ears. Thus they remained some time—in suspense. They could hear talking, yonder ; but neither was able to guess who it was.

All of a sudden there came, on the wind, a long, tremulous, plaintive bleat.

Don Marchino struck the table with his fist, shaking all over with rage.

" It's she ! Again ! " he said. " But what does that woman want of me ? What can I do for her ? "

And he asked Rosa, who at that moment came

in again : " Lodgings ? the ass ? what does she want ? "

Rosa shook her head : " She says, will you please be so good as to give her a blessing ? "

Don Marchino fell from the clouds.

" A blessing ? on whom ? on her ? did she say a blessing ? what sort of a blessing ? Go, bring her in ! but alone ! she is quite capable of dragging her nanny-goat and child in here. . . . A blessing at this hour ! "

Nunziata came in barefoot, adjusting her hair, which had been dishevelled by the wind. On seeing that little quiet room in the house of her old *curato* (1), which reminded her of former times, she withdrew her hands from her head to her face and began to weep. Whereupon Marianna asked about her husband, if he really was so ill, and she nodded affirmatively.

" But is it a hopeless case ? "

" It doesn't seem to have quite come to that," she answered. " Yet " . . . and she shook her head, not in desolation though, but rather with a flash of hatred in her tearful eyes.

" I know who it was ! " she cried. " It was here, here that they put the evil eye on me ! They knew I was happy and unruffled . . . and it wasn't enough for them to put it on my husband; they went and put it on my little boy and on the only bit of an animal I had left, which I minded like the apple of my eye because it gave me milk for him. . . . Oh, wretches ! wretches ! "

1. Cp. the French *curé*.

Until a short while ago—she related—that goat, bought for nine crowns, was the envy of everybody. Now while the boy was tending her at the pasture, she had suddenly taken fright. Both of them, the boy and the goat, had come home in the evening ' frighted,' and since then there had been a continual wasting away : " The boy . . . oh, you should see him, out there, what he has come to, and the goat . . . the goat is worse than the boy ! " No one had wanted her at the fair, not even for two crowns. Don Marchino must, for charity's sake, bless them both that very evening.

" But you have your own *curato*, now, at Sorìfa ! " sourly remarked Don Marchino. " No, you, you are my *curato* ! " entreated Nunziata. " And I want them blessed here, because the evil eye came from here : I know it, I know it ! "

Don Marchino tried to show her that the evil eye was a foolish superstition, and that if she was laying it at the door of the youth with whom she courted as a girl, why there ! let her think no more about it, because he . . . But no ! Nunziata wouldn't say to whom she put it down. She wanted the blessing, that's what she wanted.

" But, at this hour ? " repeated Don Marchino, fuming.

Again, borne on the wind, came the tremulous bleating of the goat.

" Do you hear her ? " said Nunziata. " Please ! "

" Well, but not both of them ! " protested

Don Marchino. " It's a long business, my dear, and it's already late. You can imagine ! I was preparing to go to bed ! Come, hurry up ! either the goat or the boy : who needs it most ? "

" The boy," answered Nunziata quickly. " He's lying like a rag out there, on the bench in front of the chapel. Oh ! what I have gone through, my dear Don Marchino, to drag him up here, partly on his feet and partly on these arms that I can hardly feel any more ! "

Don Marchino flew into a passion : " But how can one think, how can one think, I say, of taking a boy in that state to Nocera ? "

" Why because the goat, Don Marchino "— Nunziata hastened to explain—" the goat won't go a step without him. The little thing feels that they are both joined together in the same calamity and it calls him, speaks to him and doesn't want to move away from him."

" That's enough. So, the boy ? " concluded Don Marchino.

Nunziata stood thinking perplexedly. Then she said : " If you won't do it for both . . ."

" No ! for both, no ; we have said : either one or the other."

" Well, then . . . bless the goat, so that it can at least give milk for my Gigi again."

On going outside into the wind, into the darkness of the stormy night, she first turned her eyes to the bench on which her son had curled himself up to sleep.

" Gildino . . ." she called.

The boy did not answer. She then felt strangely dismayed at the sight of a Nature almost entirely in flight amidst the howling vehemence of the wind. Across the sky torn clouds, in endless numbers, were flying in desperate fury and seemed to draw the moon along with them ; the trees writhed and creaked, sighing ceaselessly as it to uproot themselves and fly thither, thither where the wind was carrying the clouds, to a tempestuous gathering. She unloosed the goat, which had been tied to the trunk of a tree, and waited some time at the door of the chapel ; because Don Marchino wished first to finish his glass without hurrying, and then he had to put on his cassock again and get the book, the aspergill, and the little oil lamp. The goat could not go inside the church. The blessing had to be done there, in front of the door. Don Marchino opened half of it, from within, and placed the lamp on a crosspiece of the other half in order to shelter it from the wind. The woman, holding the goat round the neck, knelt down in front of that small, flickering light.

" We shall have to manage like this," said the priest.

" Yes, Don Marchino ; but please do it well."

" Good heavens, do you think I would do it badly ? I'm doing it just as it's written here in the book."

And with his glasses astride the tip of his nose he began to miaou the adjuration. Now and again the goat bleated and turned its head towards the bench on which the boy was lying. At a certain point Don Marchino interrupted himself : " Do you hear, eh ? *a malis oculis, a malis oculis,* which means precisely : from the evil eye."

She, who was accompanying on her knees that adjuration by praying with the most intense fervour, nodded several times at his interruption to let him know that she had understood. Yes, yes, *a malis oculis, a malis oculis.* . . .

When the blessing was over, Don Marchino hastened to close the chapel door, on the excuse of the wind being liable to blow out the lamp. And he left the woman outside still on her knees. But he hadn't yet passed from the chapel into the presbytery when he heard a shriek, a howling as of a wounded beast, out in the square. His sister and the maid came to him frightened.

" What else is the matter ? " cried Don Marchino. " Now, listen, I'm not going to give myself any more trouble, even if the world falls to pieces ! "

But alas ! he had to trouble himself, because that night the whole of Stravignano came out at the cries of that unfortunate woman, who had found her son dead on the bench ; and this time Don Marchino even had to lend his ass to those who charitably offered to take the little corpse to Sorìfa. Waddling about on his bow legs among the crowd, ruffled in the wind, he kept saying : " And 'struth ! she wanted me to bless the goat and not the boy ! "

But as they all indignantly turned away from him, he craned his neck, opened out his hands fanwise before his chest, and, turning down the corners of his mouth, repeated : " I can't make people out ! "

> From *Novelle per un anno*, vol. 8. R. Bemporad, Firenze, 1925. (First published in *The Bermondsey Book*, March 1926.)

THE STARLING AND THE ANGEL ONE-HUNDRED-AND-ONE

WE had risen while it was still dark and had been walking for three hours as hungry as wolves, taking certain villainous short cuts which, according to Stefano Traìna, ought to have saved us a third of the distance ; but we had already been obliged to turn back two or three times, being unable to find any way out, and I do not know how much time we had lost climbing over old walls, wading across pebbly brooks and making our way through thick hedges of cacti and brambles. These hard labours had robbed us of the only real compensation for our lost sleep : that of enjoying the exhilarating freshness of the morning air in the country, while we walked along level roads. Who of us, in such circumstances, could have had the spirit to contradict Stefano Traìna and defend the starlings, which he depicted as being a real calamity to the country, much worse even than that true scourge of God, the locust-fly ?

But Stefano Traìna was like that : when speaking he felt the need of believing that someone was contradicting him ; and growing all the time more heated, he wanted to make us three poor innocents believe the starlings came in such thick clouds that in passing over the sun they obscured it, and that if they should descend on a wood of olive trees, in the twinkling of an eye they would exterminate it. Because it appeared that each starling carried away with him no less than three olives, one in each claw and another in his beak, and that he would swallow them whole, digesting them as though they were a mere nothing.

" Stone and all ? " asked Bartolino Gaglio, astounded.

" Stone and all."

" On my soul ! What a digestion ! " exclaimed Sebastiano Terilli.

" The starlings ? Why I tell you . . ." went on Stefano Traìna. In conclusion, he showed that if on the one hand we ought to thank Celestino Calandra, the youngest and handsomest of the canons of Montelusa, for having invited us to spend a week on his lands at Cumbo, on the other hand Celestino Calandra ought to be very grateful to us for the signal service we were going to render him in saving his crop of olives by shooting the starlings. It is true that neither I nor Sebastiano Terilli nor Bartolino Gaglio had ever done any shooting, as could be seen by the bright newness of our guns, bought only the day before. But this did not really matter. According to Stefano Traìna, one could shoot starlings even with one's eyes shut.

Well, it may have been because we shot with only one eye shut and the other open, but the fact is that after four days of the most relentless chase in the olive woods of Cumbo, not a starling worth calling one did we succeed in bringing down, not even by accident ; but olives, oh yes, they fell like hail at every shot : to such an extent that the good Celestino Calandra (who was young and saintly) began to remark, between gentle laughs, that it could not be other than God himself who sent him such a consolation.

Extermination there was, but that was in the poultry-yards of Cumbo. A pantagruelian hunger arose in all four of us young hunters ; but perhaps it was only rage that possessed us, and this on account of all the starlings we had failed to hit and which flew away so quietly, without the slightest haste, as if they would have said : " Ugh, how annoying you are with your shots ! "

Celestino Calandra's housekeeper, Donna Gesa (who was old and saintly) holding, one in each hand, two bunches of chickens with necks drawn and heads dangling, looked daggers at us each morning when we returned from our shoot-

ing, and more especially at Sebastiano Terilli,
who not content with the destruction of olive
trees and of chickens, irritated *Monsignore* at
table with his arguments on matters which were
neither here nor there. The good odour of
the country house buried in the midst of olive
and almond trees, those patriarchal rooms,
bare, ample and resounding, with their uneven
floors that smelt of stored grain, of must, of the
sweat of those who labour in the sun and of the
smoke from the burning of straw and wood in
the rude fireplaces : all these things did not
succeed in softening Sebastiano Terilli's acrid
spirit, dilettante philosopher and convinced
materialist that he was.   It is true he apostroph-
ised the soul in almost every one of his frequent
exclamations : " By the soul of this, by the soul
of that " ; but he did not really mean the ' soul,'
it was merely a mode of expression.

The most heated discussions were those which
took place in the evening, after supper ; and they
very much disturbed Donna Gesa, the old
housekeeper, whose habit it was before going to
bed to bundle herself up warmly and retire to a
corner of the dining-room in order to tell her
rosary of fifteen ' decades.' They very much
disturbed her, because she felt continually
tempted to interrupt and to contradict, as could
plainly be seen by her gestures, the grimaces
that she made, and the rapid rubbing of a finger
every now and then under her disdainful nose.

She was a little woman, thin and active, always

slightly irritable. Between her long thin lips there was generally to be seen a light froth of saliva. Her eyelids blinked continually over her sharp little dark eyes, like a ferret's ; and on her cheeks, between her temples and her nose and just below the skin, there stretched an intricate network of tiny violet-coloured veins.

Finally, one morning after breakfast, she could stand it no longer. We were talking about women, the choice of wives, and mothers and daughters-in-law. Stefano Traìna, who had in his house a terror of a mother-in-law, burst into an angry tirade against the whole tribe. " But very often," Donna Gesa suddenly rejoined with upraised hands and quivering nostrils, " very often it is the daughters-in-law who are vipers ! Vipers, yes, vipers ! And yet it is always the mothers-in-law who are blamed ! " Stefano Traìna gazed at her for a moment as though petrified ; then, jumping to his feet, he ran to his room, seized his gun and rushed out of the house.

We all broke into loud laughter. But Donna Gesa only frowned, and waited until we had finished ; then turning to *Monsignore* and gently shaking her head in sign of commiseration, she asked : " Wasn't that old Donna Poponè a good creature ? Your Reverence knows she was : the one in the miracle of the Angel One-hundred-and-one." " Tell us about it ! Tell us about it ! " we cried, Bartolino Gaglio and I. But Sebastiano Terilli, interposing with noisy in-

credulity, demanded : " One moment ! Wait a
moment ! What is that you said ? One-
hundred-and-one ? Is there then a hundredth
and a hundred-and-first angel ? "

" Of course there is ! " exclaimed Bartolino
Gaglio immediately, fearing the interruption
might make the old woman indignant and
unwilling to tell the story. " The hundred-and-
first, the hundred-and-second, the hundred-and-
third. . . . What is there to marvel at in that ?
There are the angels, and God assigns to each
one his own number."

Celestino Calandra (who was young and
saintly) smiled good-humouredly and explained
to us that in this case the number one hundred
and one was not, strictly speaking, a progressive
number, but that it referred to a particular angel
to whom the people of the neighbourhood were
especially devoted, as to one who had under his
charge a hundred of the souls in Purgatory,
leading them every night to holy enterprises.

" A centurion angel, then ? " suggested
Terilli.

" Well now, what about old Donna Poponè ? "
I asked, annoyed, and turning to Donna Gesa.
Whereupon she sat down, and began to relate.

" Her real name was Maragrazia Aiello.
Poponè was only a nickname, but all the Aiellos,
from father to son, have been so called—who can
tell why ?

" Long-suffering as an angel, she always went

about with downcast eyes, poor thing, and with
sealed lips. What was hers did not belong to
her. She had deprived herself of everything for
the sake of her son, and now remained where she
was put without giving annoyance to anyone, not
even to the air.

" But her daughter-in-law, who was called
Maricchia, offered her provocation upon provocation from morning till evening. Oh, the brazen
face of her which never blushed at anything, her
wagging tongue and forward character !

" There is nothing worse than a forward
woman. She would not wear the *mantellina* like
all the other women of the village, because she
said her father was a master-workman ; she wore,
instead, the wool *manto*, cut into points and
fringed. She also wished to be called *'gnora* and
not *comare* (1).

" Donna Poponè kept silent and suffered all
these things for love of her son, who was also
rather easy-going—rather tame indeed. If he
had been my son ! However. What did she not
endure, that poor creature of God, Donna Poponè !

" At sixty years of age you ought to have seen
her—without a single white hair. She was like a
little waxen madonna : spotlessly clean and neat,
with thick hair and fresher in complexion than a
girl of fifteen. Like all poor women, she dressed
in barracan (2) ; but on her any ugly old thing

1. *'gnora*, a common abbreviation of *signora*. *Comare*
means ' comrade,' and corresponds to the Scottish ' cummer.'
2. A coarse cloth made of goat's hair.

seemed to be of silk, so fine a deportment had she, with something in her manner so well-bred that everyone she met immediately made way for her. I remember her hands, how fine they were : as delicate as the film of an onion. And how they had worked, those hands !

" It was not as if her daughter-in-law was at all out of pocket on her account ; because while still living she had given up to her son all that she possessed, which was a little cottage and a small plot of land under the Fornaci. She still kept herself, however, by doing *novenae* and telling rosaries for the devout who came from miles and miles to see her and who rewarded her for the blessings which she succeeded in obtaining for them from the holy souls in Purgatory, with whom during the night she was always in communion.

" Every day there were fresh proofs of this. I know this : that once a poor mother came to consult her about a son of hers who was in America and had not written for three months. ' Come again to-morrow,' said Donna Poponè. The next day she announced that the son had not written because he was on his way home, that he had already arrived at Genoa, and that in a very few days he would be with her again. And so it was. I tell you my flesh still creeps when I think of it.

" A saint ! A saint ! She was really a saint, that Donna Poponè ! "

" But what about this miracle of the Angel

One-hundred-and-one ? " asked Sebastiano Terilli.

" We are coming to that now," replied Donna Gesa.

" One day, in order to enjoy a short respite from the daily provocations of her daughter-in-law, Donna Poponè thought of going for a few weeks to the neighbouring village of Favara, where she had a sister, a widow like herself.

" She asked leave of her son, and having obtained it went to a friend in the village who was called *zi*' (1) Lisi, to ask him to lend her a little she-ass that he possessed, which was old and rather mangy, but as quiet as a tortoise. Donna Poponè knew very well that *zi*' Lisi would not refuse his ass to her, although he had no peace all day, such was his affection for the little animal, if in the morning she did not drink the whole of her usual bucketful of water. He was a strange old man, this *zi*' Lisi, and in the neighbourhood he was everywhere ridiculed on account of that little ass of his. Every morning he held up with both hands the bucket of water to the ass's nose, inviting her to drink by whistling, and sometimes this went on for an hour ⌐ two ; but woe to any of his neighbours if, annoyed by his continual, doleful whistling, they cried out to him to stop ! A widower, just as Donna Poponè was a widow, he had for many years been trying to induce her to marry him. ' Be quiet, good man ! ' Donna

1. An abbreviation of *zio*—uncle. It corresponds to ' gaffer.'

Poponè had always responded in a low voice, at the
same time making the sign of the cross, as it
seemed to her nothing less than a temptation of
the Devil.

"That day she waited in front of the small
cobblestoned court where *zi'* Lisi lived and had
his stable—waiting a long time for the old man
to finish his whistling, amidst the impatient
remarks of all the neighbours, who urged her to
enter, crying : ' Go in, go in ; if you go in he
will stop it ! ' At last the old man left off, and
then she entered the court.

"The little ass ? Certainly ! He would lend
it to her even for a month, even for a year ; he
would give it to her, and everything else besides,
all that he possessed, if . . .

"' What ! Again, you foolish old thing ?
Be quiet ! I want it only for a week ; I am going
to see my sister at Favara.'

"As soon as *zi'* Lisi heard her utter the name
' Favara,' he became very excited and began
to say that never, never, would he consent to her
going alone to that murderous place, where to
kill a man was the same as to kill a fly. And he
told her how once a Favarese, to see if his gun was
in good condition, went to the street door and
discharged it at the first person he saw passing ;
also, that a carter of Favara, after having allowed
a little boy of twelve whom he had met at midnight
on the highroad to mount up into his cart, had
killed him in his sleep because he had heard the
jingling of three *soldi* in his pocket ; he had

slaughtered him like a sheep, poor little one, put the three *soldi* into his own pocket to buy tobacco with, thrown the little corpse behind the hedge, and then, Gee up ! He had gone on, taking his time and singing as he went, beneath the stars of Heaven and under the eyes of God which were watching him. But the little soul of the poor murdered boy had cried out for vengeance, and God so disposed the mind of the carter that he himself, on arriving soon after daybreak at Favara, instead of going to his master's cart-yard, stopped in front of the Guard House and, with the three *soldi* still in his blood-stained hand, had denounced himself as though Another were speaking through his mouth.

" ' You see what God can do ! ' said Donna Poponè. ' Therefore I need have no fear.' *Zi'* Lisi tried to insist on accompanying her, but she remained firm and said that in that case she would hire somebody else's ass ; so that at last he gave in and promised her that next day at dawn the little ass would be standing in front of her door, pack-saddle and all. Now it happened, during the night, that zi' Lisi, having on his mind the ass which was to be ready by dawn, woke up. It was bright moonlight, and to him it seemed to be day. So he jumped from his bed, saddled the little ass while you could say ' Amen,' and leading her to Donna Poponè's, knocked at the door and said : ' The little ass is here, *'gna* (1)

1. Another abbreviation very widely used in Central Italy : *'Gna = Compagna*, another form of *Comare*.

Poponè. I have tied her to the ring. May the
Saviour and His blessed Mother accompany
you ! '

" Very softly, so as not to waken her daughter-
in-law, her son and her little grandchildren,
Donna Poponè began to dress herself. But,
accustomed as she was to rise at the break of
dawn, she could not convince herself in the silence
which reigned everywhere around her that it
was really time to set out on her journey. ' Yet
it must be ! ' she said to herself. ' My sleep
has deceived me.'

" So she went out with her bundle under her
mantellina. But, on looking at the sky, she
noticed immediately that it was not the brightness
of dawn which she saw, but only the light of
the moon. The whole countryside was sleeping
peacefully ; even the little ass slept, on her feet,
tied there to the ring near the door.

" ' Oh, Jesu,' exclaimed Donna Poponè, ' how
stupid that *zi'* Lisi is !   Must I now start on my
journey by night ?   Well, well, I am old, there
is the moon and I have nothing to lose.   Besides,
the holy souls from Purgatory will accompany
me.'

" She mounted the ass, and making the sign
of the cross set out on her journey.   When she
was already a good way from the village and
surrounded by the open country, moving along
slowly on the little ass in the moonlight, she
began to think of the boy who had been murdered
and thrown behind the dusty hedge, poor little

creature of God, and of the many other crimes
and wicked vendettas that were told about
Favara, meanwhile riding on with her *mantellina*
over her head and pulled down to her eyes to
prevent herself from seeing the frightening
shadows in the country on either side of the road,
where the dust lay so thick that not even the hoofs
of the little ass could be heard.

" Her journey in that great silence, on that
long, white road under the moonlight : it all
seemed to her like a dream.

" ' Oh, ye holy souls in Purgatory,' she kept
saying to herself, ' I commend myself to you.'
And not for a moment did she cease to pray.

" But either on account of the slowness of her
progress or because of her weakness or for
whatever reason, at last she was overcome by
sleep. Donna Poponè could not quite say how
it was, but the fact is that waking up at a certain
point she found herself between two long files of
soldiers, one on either side of the road ; and at
their head, in the middle of the road, was their
captain riding on his horse.

" At this sight, Donna Poponè felt quite
comforted, and she thanked God that just on
the very night of her journey He had so provided
that those soldiers should also be going to Favara.
What rather astonished her, however, was that
so many young men of about twenty years of
age said not a word on seeing in their midst an
old woman like herself, on an ass that seemed even
older than she was and which certainly could not

have cut a very fine figure on the highroad at
such an hour.   But why were they so silent, all
these soldiers ?   Even their tread could not be
heard, nor did they raise the slightest dust.
Donna Poponè now looked at them quite awe-
struck, not knowing indeed what to think.   They
seemed like shadows in the moonlight, and yet
they were real, yes, real soldiers, and there was
their captain on his horse.   But why were they so
silent ?

    " She understood why, when, at daybreak,
she came in sight of the village.   At a certain
point the captain stopped his horse and waited
for Donna Poponè to come up to him.   ' Maragrazia Aiello,' he then said to her, ' I am the
Angel One-hundred-and-one to whom you are
so devoted, and these who have escorted you thus
far are souls from Purgatory.   As soon as you
arrive, make your peace with God, because before
midday you will die.'   Thus he spoke, and vanished together with the holy escort.

    " When the sister at Favara saw Donna
Poponè arrive at her house as pale as wax and
with fixed, staring eyes, she cried :

    " ' What is the matter, Maragrà ? '

    " ' Call me a confessor,' answered the other
with a ghost of a voice.

    " ' Do you feel ill ? '

    " ' I must make my peace with God.   Before
midday I shall die.'

    " And so in fact it was.   Before midday she
died.   And all the people of Favara came out

of their houses to see the saint whom the Angel
One-hundred-and-one and the souls from
Purgatory had that night escorted up to the gates
of the village."

Donna Gesa finished speaking. Her master,
Monsignore, Gaglio and I, remained silent in
admiration ; but Sebastiano Terilli, shaking
himself, exclaimed :

" By my soul, what a miracle ! Is that the
miracle ? But what miracle is that ? Excuse
me. . . . A miracle ? Why a miracle ? We
will admit everything : we will admit that the
old woman did not die of fear, and that she was
not the victim of a hallucination, which would
be nevertheless quite understandable in one who
believed that every night she talked to the souls
in Purgatory and to this Angel One-hundred-
and-one. We will even admit that the angel
really appeared and spoke to her. What then ?
Far from being a miracle, it was nothing but an
act of the greatest cruelty to announce to a poor
old woman her imminent death ! Why, excuse
me, we all of us only live on condition that . . ."

Celestino Calandra here stretched out his hand
to reply, and that eternal discussion began again
with even greater vehemence than before.

But the faith, the faith ! Must we not take
into consideration the faith with which these poor
people sustain and comfort themselves ? So-
called intellectual men do not perceive, are
unable to perceive, anything but life, and never

give a thought to death. Science, discoveries, fame and power are what they seek ; and they ask themselves how the ignorant poor, those who dig the ground and seem to be condemned to the hardcst and most humble labours, manage to live without all these great and fine things : how they manage to live and why ; meanwhile despising them as being no better than the brutes. Little do they know that a higher spiritual truth, compared with which all the great discoveries of science, the dominion of the world and the glory of the arts become nothing but vain and foolish trifles, dwells as a most unshaken conviction in those simple souls and renders death as desirable to them as a just reward.

Who knows how long this discussion about the miracle of the Angel One-hundred-and-one might have continued, if another miracle, and this time a true, authentic, unquestionable one, had not suddenly cut it short. Stefano Traìna, with his shot-gun in his hand, burst into the dining-room breathless and exultant, his face flushed, scratched, smudged and purple with excitement. . . .

He had succeeded at last in killing a starling !

From *Novelle per un anno*, vol. 8. R. Bemporad, Firenze, 1925. (First published in *The Bermondsey Book*, June 1927.)

PANZINI

ALFREDO PANZINI was born at Senigallia near
Ancona, on the Adriatic coast, in 1863.   He
studied first at Venice, and later under Carducci,
at Bologna.   Here he took his degree in 1887.
He then became master in a *ginnasio* at Milan,
where he remained until 1917, when he was
called to Rome to teach in the *Istituto Superiore
di Magistero* and to act as inspector of elementary
schools.   He is also Honorary Professor of
Italian Literature in the University of Bologna.

His life has been quiet and uneventful, and
his literary genius slow in developing.   He was
already thirty years old when he wrote his first
work of any importance : *Il libro dei morti*.   His
principal works, in order of publication, are :
Il libro dei morti (1893), *L'evoluzione di Giosuè
Carducci* (1894), *Gli ingenui* (1896), *Piccole
storie del Mondo grande* (1901), *Lepida et tristia*
(1902), *Dizionario moderno* (1905), *Le fiabe della
virtù* (1905), *Da Plombières a Villafranca* (1909),
La lanterna di Diogene (1909), *Cos'è l'amore*
(1912), *Santippe* (1914), *Donne, madonne e bimbi*
(1915), *Il romanzo della guerra* (1915), *La
madonna di Mamà* (1916), *Novelle d'ambo i sessi*
(1918), *Il viaggio di un povero letterato* (1919),
Io cerco moglie (1920), *Il mondo è rotondo* (1921),
Il diavolo nella mia libreria (1921), *Il padrone
sono me* (1922), *La vera istoria dei tre colori* (1924),
La pulcella senza pulcellaggio (1925), *Le damigelle*
(1926), *I tre re con Gelsomino buffone del re* (1927).

53

FATHER AND SON

SIGNOR DOMENICO knew exactly how many yoke of oxen were in his stables ; how many sacks of grain he had thrashed ; how much money he had in the Savings-bank ; but he scarcely ever remembered that he had also a son.

" Your father's oxen are gayer and fatter than you are," Marco's friends would tell him. Because Signor Domenico was an excellent cattle breeder ; and when, with their slow steps, his oxen went down to the city fair, their horns would be wound about with fine, nodding tassels of brilliant red wool, which fell over their white foreheads.

" And isn't he right ? " said a merry friend ; " a yoke of oxen bring him in a fine profit—but you, Marco, how much does your father make out of you by the end of the year ? "

If casually opening a newspaper, Signor Domenico chanced upon the name of his son mentioned there, such a fury of disgust would seize him, that for all that day he was even harder than usual at the fair ; and the dealers could do nothing with him, as he would be quite capable, for half a ' marengo,' (1) of neither selling nor buying.

" Well, Signor Domenico, have you noticed that to-day your son is criticising the King ?

1. A gold coin worth twenty *lire*, stamped at the time of Napoleon and named after the battle of Marengo.

And only yesterday he was criticising the Socialists. He has no respect for anybody ! ''

This was a bitter mouthful for Signor Domenico
to swallow at the tavern, after the fatigues of the
market.

" Do you call him *my* son ? " he would demand.
" He is rather a son of a . . ." and then he
would utter a very ugly word.

Even Marco had said to him : " There is
nothing of you in me, father—you may forget
me without remorse."

He was entirely the son of his mother—a
superior and sensitive woman, whom Signor
Domenico, owing to a strange freak of passion,
had married when he was very young and by
whom he had had that only son, Marco. After
many years of union, husband and wife had
parted—like two wayfarers who are scarcely
on speaking terms—she by the way of death ;
he following the road of his business and
markets.

And when sometimes he thought of his dead
wife, he would say :

" She was a mare of ' English ' breed. . . .
For my service, there was wanted a wife of
tougher stock." " Of course," as he often
repeated while she was still living, " Get wives
and oxen from your own country." (1)

1. A Northern Italian adage, closely akin to the well-known
Tuscan : " Donne e buoi dei paesi tuoi," *i.e.* " Get women and
oxen from your own country."

However, Signor Domenico did not take another wife ; he said he did not wish to tempt Providence by a second marriage. And he kept to his word, although he was yet a young man with scarcely any white hairs showing in his strong black beard.

Perhaps Marco was grateful that no one had been put in his mother's place ; but he never said so. He never even mentioned to his father the name of his mother, for whom he cherished a feeling of deep and loyal veneration ; although he was still a child when she died—leaving him as a memento of her only his thoughtful eyes, and a white lock almost hidden in the dark masses of his hair. Otherwise he resembled his father in outward appearance, being dark, and hairy, with a masterful nose under a permanent line in the middle of his forehead.

When his wife died, Signor Domenico put his son to college in the neighbouring town. And every Saturday, when he went down from ' Cipressina ' (1) to the market, he would go to see him, taking some little present : nuts, green almonds, or a big bunch of grapes plucked along with the leaves ; according, in short, to the time of the year.

And the little student priests, and also the grown ones, would often say to him :

" What a genius your little Marco is ! After reading a page from a book just once, he is

1. The nearest English equivalent would be ' Cypress Farm.'

able to repeat it all from memory—it is really astonishing ! "

So that when Marco left college, Signor Domenico ingenuously asked his son's friends :

" Is it really true that my son is a genius, as they say ? "

Because people would stop him on purpose to remark :

" What a mind that son of yours has ! "

" Perhaps too much of it for his years " . . . a grave and important personage had once said to him.

" Very good, *s'avì d'l'inzegn*, if you have genius in you, why then, out with it ! " said the father, apostrophising his absent son.

And for years and years he waited, expecting the fruits of his son's genius to appear, as the husbandman looks forward to seeing the full ears of corn.

But his son Marco's intellectual growth was of a hidden nature. He was a great fencer with words, and was quite capable of remaining at the café until break of dawn, if he found an adversary worthy to cross swords with him ; even in useless discussion.

People would admiringly recount to Signor Domenico how they had stayed until a very late hour listening to his son, who was disputing with the others.

What had they been talking about ? Who had won ? This they could not tell him ; but

Marco's opinion was always different from that of all the others : this they did know.

" And mind you "—they would say to Signor Domenico—" it takes something to make people lose their night's rest ; and that without wine or women ! "

" If he has this great gift of talking," Signor Domenico thought to himself, after some pulling at his beard, " let us hope he will become a great lawyer."

But although his son Marco certainly became Doctor of Laws, he did not become a lawyer.

Instead, he began to write books.

One of Marco's friends told Signor Domenico that they had once tried to find a subject which his son did not understand ; " but it was really marvellous—he seemed to know everything."

From that time a grave suspicion was born in Signor Domenico's heart, and he pulled at his beard more thoughtfully than ever, thinking sorrowfully to himself :

" I am very much afraid there is one thing which he does not understand, and that is : life."

And as time went on he became yet more confirmed in this opinion, so that an ever-increasing contempt for his son began to grow in his heart.

Also, in the presence of his farm hands he got into the habit of saying :

" My son is like a cow which they sold to me as being with calf. I waited patiently while she ate and ate ; but time went on, and no calf

was forthcoming ! Whatever could it be ?
Instead of a calf, she had a swelling, a disease of
some sort ! ! "

And the countrymen would laugh at their
master's wit, because even he was clever, in his
own way.

His son knew all about these comparisons,
and other things besides ; but he did not allow
his scorn to show itself too much—he only said :

" I am sorry for you, father."

Avoiding all discussion, he would say sweetly,
almost affectionately :

" I am very sorry for you, father."

Sorry for him ? Didn't he know that if anyone else had said that, he—his father—had still
spunk enough to throw him out of the window ?

" Bring another bottle ! "

And on the servant's bringing another bottle,
Signor Domenico would sit alone, drinking, and
frowning more and more, until the bottle was
empty and darkness had fallen.

His son only drank water.

Such scenes were rare, and became even rarer ;
because little by little, Marco drew away from
his father's house and came but seldom to
' Cipressina.'

But when he did come, although Signor
Domenico was a good host and his son's room was
always in order and ready for him, his father
felt the need of speaking his mind ; so that when
they found themselves opposite to each other,

with the soup-tureen between them, and were just tasting the first mouthfuls, Signor Domenico would begin :

"Very good : I am only an ignoramus, a cattle-merchant, while you are a talented and superior person—agreed : but wait a moment ! Do you know how to make bank-notes of a thousand ? No ! It was your father's business to make those for you. You wished to study in order to become a Doctor of Laws—very well— but you refuse to be a lawyer because you say you do not wish to deceive your fellows—well, let that pass also—although you might have thought of it before. Will you accept a salaried post of some kind ? Again, no ! Because you are intolerant of all discipline and have a difficult character. . . . Mind, your friends themselves say you have a difficult character. . . . You could have gained the vote of the proletariat here, but you allowed that to be carried off by the Honourable ——.

"I know all about that night at the café, when you got him with his back to the wall and left him without a rag to cover himself, as the saying is. How they applauded you ! 'What a clever fellow your son is !' Of course ; they came on purpose to tell me so. But afterwards ? After- wards, when the lights were out at the café, and the sun had risen once more ? The Honourable —— became member of Parliament, and in only two years has made a position for himself, desper- ate as his situation was. Now he rides in a motor-car ; and when the peasants ask : ' How is it, your Honour, that you ride in a motor-car, and we still go on foot ? ' he replies : ' To serve you the quicker, my friends ! ' Now that, for instance, is what I call clever ; and he is exactly the same age as you—thirty-six. But as to this writing of books ! Do you ever sell your books ? Haven't we here, in the house, a shop-full of them ? Every book that you publish is a disaster, another yoke of good oxen vanished into air, that is to say, at the price of cattle to-day, another couple of notes of a thousand ! "

Signor Domenico knew it was not kind to speak like this, but he felt the need of saying certain things, if only to make his son reply to them. Because to him, to him alone, this great talker did not deign to give an answer. Did his son think him a fool ? Were not his reasons just ?

On one occasion, Marco had answered him, saying :

" Father, I have outgrown all the illusions and superstitions of this life."

" Then you are ' out ' as they say in the game of ' Seven and a half ' (1). You have gone out of life. Pay up ! " retorted the father.

On another occasion, Marco had said, almost as if reproving his father's avarice :

" I would give one of your notes of a thousand just for an idea ! "

1. A game of cards, very popular in Northern and Central Italy. Seven points and a half is ' game,' but he who scores more than seven and a half is ' out ' and has to pay a forfeit.

"Ah, you despise my good money then? But let me tell you, one of your ideas will not even make the pot boil!"

"Do you grudge me the bread I eat here?" And, pushing his plate violently from him, he got up and walked slowly away.

His father watched him, tall, bent and sad, walking round and round the garden of 'Cipressina,' almost as if his mind were chained to that spot.

"Look how nearly forty years have been wasted!" bemoaned Signor Domenico, filled more with pity than with anger at the thought of how little respect Marco had for him. Yet again he remembered certain words of his son's, which some friends had reported to him. Marco had said:

"If it were not for my father, I should be obliged to earn my bread as a carter!"

Then if even he could see reason, why was he so obstinate?

"You have this disease of writing books? Very well, but why write books which are read only by two people, yourself and the printer?"

Signor Domenico knew it was not kind to say this, but he did it with the best intentions. As a father, he was able to say what no one else would have the courage to tell Marco, to his face.

"Look at that literary friend of yours!" he went on. "He also writes books, but they are nice spicy books. Besides he is always as trim and well-mannered as a poodle ; and has been able to fish for himself a substantial marriage dowry. But as for you ! You are like one of those dogs who have no master ; you are up against everybody—even the women ! Did you make this world ? No. Well then ? Quarrel with God Almighty, because He didn't send for you to ask your opinion as to how it should be done ! "

"Don't you understand," and Signor Domenico lowered his voice as if about to say something very profound, " don't you understand that you should never speak ill of anybody, unless you are sure of giving pleasure to somebody else ? "

" I write for those yet to come."

" For those yet to come ? " A certain effort was necessary for the cattle-merchant even to understand these words ; but after frowning heavily for a while, Signor Domenico understood at last, and laughed until the bottles reeled on the table. " Then you really believe that the men ' yet to come ' will be different from those of to-day ? Poor fellow ! Men—and don't you forget it—are to be caught either with honey or with tongs ; and this is as true to-day as it was yesterday or will be to-morrow. But you, you can't do it—neither with honey, nor with tongs ! Oh, if only you could, even I would cry ' bravo ! ' If I knew that you could take men as the builder takes his bricks—breaking them with the hammer and plastering them with cement ; and then, ' Stick there, you rascal ! ' That is what I

would like to see !   Not this shutting yourself
up for a couple of months in your room to write ;
not this walking about the fields like a dreamer,
talking with Dante and that other . . . !   Who
is that other fellow ?   Shame on you to throw
away your life like that !   Do you want to know
why you write ?   Would you like me to tell
you ?"

"Oh, do not scruple to tell me that also !"
said Marco, his white, trembling lips widening
into a smile.

"Because of the monstrous pride which devours
you !"

This time it was the father who got up and left
the table ; and a long look of hatred passed between the two men.

"Yes, yes, he does well not to come any more
—it poisoned my blood only to see him.   Let
him go away, far away into the world.   Besides,
it seemed as if he were imprisoned in this
wretched place.   They call him strong—but
how can that be, if he has the spirit of a broody
hen ?"

His father said this, because every now and
then—though indeed ever more rarely—his
son Marco would return to 'Cipressina.'

But now they no longer spoke to one
another.

Although Signor Domenico could not refrain
from remarking to his farm hands, with a
sneer :

" My son is come, to be delivered."

" Then he will win the prize of a million," (1) the men would say.

Yes, but the father was referring to another new book.

He had noticed for some time that his son was able to write his books only at ' Cipressina,' in his own room ; where he shut himself up for weeks and months together like a sitting hen : only coming out for a little in the evening, and gesticulating while he walked, as if in conversation with some invisible person.

" Keep away from him," Signor Domenico would say jokingly to his people, " because just now he is talking with Dante."

Afterwards, he heard that his son had published another book.

As usual, it was Don Geremìa, the parish priest, a man not altogether without learning, who gave the news to Signor Domenico and congratulated him on it.

" Have you bought it, Don Geremìa ? "

" No."

" Have you read it ? "

" No."

" Ah, you son of a dog," (he was the dog, but it did not matter : the word came out so easily), " if only you gambled or had some enjoyment with the money ! "

1. ' To win a million ' or ' to win the prize of a million ' is a common saying in Italy when any impossible feat is proposed or suggested.

Two years later, one evening, Marco came.

Signor Domenico was told next morning, on awaking, that his son had arrived. And when he saw Marco, he told him that he was ' welcome.'

It was a clear, fresh, September morning—and as soon as Signor Domenico had lit his favourite pipe, there arose in his heart a feeling of great satisfaction : first, because the beans and all kinds of winter crops, after a good shower of rain, were already showing green in the fields ; then, the price of cattle was still going up, and he had his stables full ; also, the value of the grape crop was rising from market to market, and his vineyards seemed really to be blessed.

So that having lit his good pipe, he had said ' welcome ' to his son, which seemed to him more than enough ; thinking at the same time : " Here is my son come again to ' Cipressina,' to be delivered of another book ! "

Which thought led naturally to the other, that it would mean a loss of about a hundred ' marenghi ' in the profits from the cattle—that is, if the book were a big one, and his son's books were usually big ones.

But passing near the cypress tree, under which his son was sitting, and noticing that he was very pale, he said to him :

" Don't you feel well ? "

Marco got up, greeted his father, and then began to walk about on long unsteady legs, avoiding the shade of the cypress trees and seeking the golden warmth of the sun.

" Are you feeling ill ? " again asked his father.

" A little exhausted ; but it will soon pass."

" You fancy," observed his father reprovingly, " that your brain is like a bullock wagon, able to carry fifty hundredweight. Instead, let me tell you, it is only a light carriage."

" It carries . . . it still carries a few hundredweights," replied Marco—but with a voice that seemed changed.

" Well ! Go on carrying your load then ! "

And Signor Domenico went off to inspect his vines. In the orchard he found the maid picking the last red pods of his beautiful Spanish beans (1). " Listen to me," he said, " let the bean-soup go for to-day. Kill a cockerel instead."

" One of the hens that are not laying would be better " . . . said the maid.

" A cockerel, I tell you ! Because the broth from a hen is too fat."

Signor Domenico relit his pipe, and turning back again, said to the maid :

" Once upon a time, you knew how to make a cream " . . . and he ordered her to make the cream ; but it was to be light, without any flour added to it, and the little flakes of puff-paste were to be made as thin as possible.

1. A variety of the scarlet-runner bean. It has white flowers and white seeds. In the United States it is also known as the ' Spanish ' bean, but is mainly cultivated for its flowers.

"Not as you like them, so that you can feel them under the teeth ? " asked the maid.

"No, as thin as possible."

But when dinner-time came, Marco did not appear.

"Can he have gone off again ? " thought his father. But passing his son's room, he noticed that his shoes had been put outside the door.

And those shoes—it was bright mid-day—taken off and thrown there, outside the door, gave him an impression, as if they had said :

"We shall do no more walking ! "

Bursting into the room, he found his son lying down still dressed, a black, gaunt and motionless figure sunk into the white bed.

"What's this ? " said Signor Domenico, almost laughing, " have you thrown yourself on your bed ? Damn it ! But you are in a raging fever ! "

"Biasin," he called from the window, " harness the mare ! "

"What for ? " growled his son, but without moving.

"To go for the doctor, of course ! "

"No ! "

"Why not ? "

"Because I have no faith in doctors." . . .

"And have I ? But one calls the doctor if only to know what one ought not to do ; and also, to give them a little business. Go, Biasin, go ! And you undress yourself ! "

"No ! "

" Why not ? "

" Because I will not ! "

Marco said this in so terrible a voice that his
father dared not insist, but remained silent.
Then the door slowly opened and the maid
appeared saying :

" The soup is getting cold, it is so nice. . . ."

" Give it to the dogs " . . . and, turning to
his son :

" Will you take a little cream ? "

There was no reply ; just as if he had heard
nothing. But when his father tried to give him
some spoonfuls of the cream, Marco aroused
himself with a shudder, thrust away the spoon,
and then fell back again.

Soon evening came ; and in the growing dusk,
those two bearded faces became confused together
as in one and the same image.

The father awaited the dawn with great
anxiety ; because it seemed to him only natural,
with the coming of daylight and the rising of the
sun, that Marco's eyes should open and that he
also should arise.

" Marco, the sun is up ; open your eyes,
open them ! " cried the father, looking at his son
—and, gazing at him, he saw Marco again as a
little child ; and there returned to his memory
Marco's first, baby words, that he had uttered
when he was a little one.

And while this image of long ago grew clearer,
he saw Marco's eyes imperceptibly closing yet
more firmly . . . and looking round in terror,

he understood that Death had entered his house, and in seizing his son had laid hands also on himself.

Often do we meet ruthless Death on the highways of this world, where funerals hinder the business of life ; and there are those among us who become impatient and even curse at this hindrance, without thinking that the pale One (1) is also on her way to us.

When Marco was dead, his father remained contemplating him for a long time : and then there came to Signor Domenico a full realisation of the great fatigue which had killed him. So that when they disputed about the cause of his death, he told them : " Of overwork." Also, when the newspapers, and people generally, wondered that so strong a man should die like that, " a man of iron," " No, only a poor child," said Signor Domenico.

Because he only had seen, through the unchanging aspect of death, the image of Marco as a little child ; and the more he gazed, the more clearly he saw the little Marco whom he had accompanied to College, and to whom he had taken presents of fruits in their seasons. A little martyr killed by an immense toil.

But this was a vision which no one else could see ; he only saw it ; and he felt himself taken by a little hand, and heard a voice saying : " Come, father ; here there is mother, too ! "

1. Cp. Horace's ' pallida mors.'

To no living man could he have told these feelings, because none would have understood.

And then he thought that one person only could have done so : she who had borne his son in her womb, and had given him that white lock amongst his black hair.

Then the father understood that he was strangely alone in the world ; and that his companions were those who were no more.

" Marco," he said softly, as if speaking to him, " Marco, I want you to write a book that will cost me the price of all my cattle ! "

He would often gaze for a long time at one spot, as if, from one moment to another, Marco were bound to appear there.

Then he began to wander a little in his mind.

After some months, Don Geremìa was surprised by this question :

" Is it true that my son is dead ? "

To which Don Geremìa answered stolidly : " We shall see him again, some day."

Afterwards, he called Don Geremìa and other priests, and gave them much money, as if to him it were a thing of no value ; not because he believed in them ; " I have no faith in you," he said ; but because it was their business, for money, to pray, to sing and to occupy themselves a good deal with the dead.

And when he heard that the newspapers were writing many things in memory of his dead son, more than they had done while he was living, he wanted to send those journalists large sums of money, that they might go on writing.

Then he wished to find a sculptor, a great sculptor, to carve the image of his son—whatever the cost might be. Only, it had to be a likeness which embodied also another hidden image, the image of a child, which should be divined through the figure of the man.

And, because a friend of Marco's, one of his merry companions at the café, had said, laughing, that Marco had died for spite at not having succeeded, and that before dying he had received the Communion just to be different from other people, Signor Domenico wanted to beat him to death, and was with great difficulty dissuaded from doing so.

Then he became much occupied with all Marco's books, papers and records ; desiring to save them from the destruction of time—for even against time would he wrestle. So he called an architect, and asked him to design a monument, which was to be all of polished marble, adorned with antique columns, and having a chamber also of finest marble, hermetically closed, in which all these relics of Marco might be preserved.

All these enterprises, in which his fine fortune was gradually wasting away, comforted him much.

But best of all was when there came to ' Cipressina ' some stranger, some philosopher, who wished to see the place where his son Marco

had lived and died.   Because there are still such
pilgrims going about this world, seeking ideas.

Then it seemed to the father as though he
were the guardian of the relics of some saint or
martyr ; for those visitors from far off lands
spoke in subdued voices and with great reverence,
as if they were on holy ground.

And one day, there came some youths from a
land beyond the Alps and beyond the sea.
They came, and one of them, who spoke Italian
with a strange and melancholy accent, made a
speech to his companions.

And while speaking he uttered a word which
among us is heard no more : ' Fatherland,' and
those youths paled in listening to him.   After
that he called on the deceased with a loud voice,
acclaiming him a hero.   And speaking of a
future, he gave the dead Marco a tryst for that
future in a distant, rugged land.

Time passed, and of Marco, the hero, there
spoke only the stones of his monument—and a
cypress tree.

From *Le fiabe della virtù*, Fratelli Treves,
Milano, 1919. (First published in
The Bermondsey Book, June 1926.)

ST. DAMIAN'S OYSTERS

THIS simple and facetious story is not about
the author, personally, but about a gentleman closely connected with him both as a blood
relation and as one for whom he cherishes great
esteem and an even greater affection ; for the
latter is a man of singular virtues, which would
be better known and appreciated in this world
if only a certain natural disdain on his part for
human errors and vanities, a melancholy habit
of living to himself and of feeding, as it were, on
his own conscience, and an unusual timidity and,
at times, harshness towards other men, did not
veil the splendour of these virtues and withhold
even their natural aroma.   But enough of him ;
let us come forthwith to the story which, to
facilitate its narration, shall be told in the first
person : but the author again gives notice that
it is not about himself, and the proof thereof
is this, that he is most temperate in food and
drink, and could sustain himself, like a *hidalgo*,
upon a handful of dried olives, while his friend
here figures as one who is given to gluttony, a
sin more displeasing than any other, as Dante
defines it in the canto of the Florentine Ciacco (1).

I was hungry that morning, more hungry than
usual : first of all because there breathed from
the clear April sky a mountain breeze which gave

1. The 6th canto of the *Inferno*.   The reference is to line
48.

one a pleasant shiver, and secondly because my luncheon hour had been delayed by a full quarter of an hour on account of my having been obliged to go to the Education Office to draw my stipend. Besides, it is incredible how much the habit of wasting some of one's breath upon school boys contributes towards the sharpening of the appetite ; and one's lungs also profit by it considerably ! That morning, moreover, I had almost allowed myself to be affected, while expounding the canto of Romeo of Provence (1) ; so that after : " And if only the world knew the heart that was in him, while bit by bit he begged his way," etc. . . . I felt a most impellent need to restore myself.

Quite so ! . . . But let us go in here : after all, it will not ruin us, once in a way. How much more will it cost ? One or two *lire*, at the very outside. And besides, have we not this day received our stipend ? *Nonne meruimus hodie stipendia ?*

Thus reasoning within myself, I bravely pushed open the glazed door of one of the most renowned and fashionable restaurants of the town, without giving any time for wise second thoughts to weaken the resolution I had made. I found myself in a magnificent hall, where beautiful divans covered with crimson velvet in front of broad tables shining with crockery and white linen invited one to be seated with every comfort.

1. The 6th canto of the *Paradiso*. The quotation is from the last triplet of this canto.

Now I must confess, that what induced me to enter that restaurant rather than another was its reputation for exquisite cookery, which I desired to confirm by personal experience. I would have ventured in there before, only I suffer from a certain aversion towards waiters, who, from above their stiff collars protruding towards their clean-shaven chins, look you up and down, read your life's history in a trice and with their eyes address you pretty much to this effect : " You are not a millionaire, you are not a nobleman, you are not a rake, you are not even a swindler : pugh ! You are to all appearances a poor, honest man, who has the greatest difficulty in making ends meet. What has blown you in here, contrary to your usual custom ? Make haste, and get out ! " And they do not say " Thank you " even if you leave on the plate a generous tip of twenty centimes.

Thus thought I, but " See human judgment, how oft it erreth ! " (1). No sooner did I appear within the hall than the proprietor (it must have been he), who was sitting at a marble desk as upon a throne, rose from his ' blessed seat ' (2) and, coming towards me, bowed most graciously and smiled upon me with the greatest deference. He was a very handsome youth, still in his adolescence, elegant, immaculately clean, as fresh as a sherbet, and so well-nourished,

1. Ariosto, *Orlando Furioso*, canto 1st, stanza 7th.
2. An allusion to Beatrice's *beato scanno* (Dante's *Inferno*, canto 2nd, line 112).

so rosy and so blooming, that he really did credit to the place.

"If the fig-peckers and quails of your restaurant have as delicate a flesh as you have, your fame is not an usurped one ; but beware, my young friend, of undertaking a voyage of discovery into unknown lands, for if, by some evil chance, you happened to fall in with the Lestrigons or with the Cannibals, I, for one, would certainly not offer any security for your return ! "

Thus did I address him—in my mind. And he, repeating his smile, made certain cabalistic signs to a waiter, who was so slender and dapper, that elsewhere I would have mistaken him for a young Honourable M.P. or for a ladies' lecturer : and yet he was only a waiter !

The latter followed me, took from me my overcoat, my hat and my stick, and led me to a secluded and almost vacant table, for at it there were only two silent Englishmen, intent upon eating, but with such perfect manners that they seemed rather to be swallowing medicinal pills. Every now and then, they would ejaculate *yes ;* and I could not but wonder how these Englishmen who eat so delicately and modestly can, on the other hand, devour nations and peoples with such voracity.

As soon as I was seated, the waiter, standing in front of me and barely resting his palms on the table, said :

" Will you begin with an appetiser of *pâté* and

truffles ? It has just come out of the ice. You will find it exquisite."

He did not actually say 'exquisite'; he said 'splendid.' In fact I can still hear him rolling this word, which he repeated in every sentence.

" Let us begin as you say ! " I replied.

" And what kind of wine would you like ? There is some very good bottled Barolo (1)."

" I do not doubt it ; but a little ordinary wine will do for me."

" Very good, Sir."

And, almost immediately, he placed before me, in a flask-stand of the brightest metal, a flask of Tuscan wine, labelled : " Very old Chianti."

" But this is too much ! " I said. " And besides, it must be very dear." . . .

" Not at all, Sir ! " replied my Ganymede. " And then, you can take just as much as you want."

So I very gently poured some of the fragrant liquor into a slender, crystal wine-glass, and upon sipping it I found that it was indeed a most choice wine ; it reminded me of the dithyramb in which Redi (2) says : " Montepulciano is the king of all wines."

1. A Piedmontese wine, so called because it comes from Barolo, near Cuneo.

2. An Italian poet of the seventeenth century, author of the famous dithyramb, " Bacchus in Tuscany " (*Bacco in Toscana*). Montepulciano, like Chianti, is a well-known Tuscan wine.

The *pâté*, also, although a piquant delicacy to which my palate was unaccustomed, seemed to me exquisitely fine, and while spreading it on the toast, I remarked to myself, that a cook who knows how to prepare such dainties certainly deserves the gratitude of his fellow men.

When I had consumed the aforesaid delicacy, the waiter reappeared and, with his gracious smile, said :

" Now I should advise you to take some soup with Bolognese dumplings ; we have had a fresh lot in this morning and they are now just done to a turn."

It did not seem to me polite to refuse so disinterested an advice, so I accepted the dumplings, which were as well received as the *pâté* and truffles had been.

" And now, Sir, I shall bring you a roast quail garnished with mushrooms."

I had already had enough, for my habitual sobriety did not exceed, at lunch, a plate of broth and a second dish ; but that *pâté* had unfortunately made more room inside, and, besides, to stop there at the soup seemed to me mean. On the other hand, it was true that the words : " A quail with mushrooms " had conjured up visions of fantastic prices not in harmony with my pocket. But the waiter, who read on my features and understood this perplexity, hastened to say :

" It's one of our special lines."

How could one say *no* ? So I likewise

accepted, and with good grace, the quail, which richly deserved its reputation and whose only fault was that it lowered the level of the wine in the flask and thereby increased a certain fogginess in my brain.

"And now that's enough, thank you !" I said to the waiter who, having removed the remains of the unfortunate quail (for nothing can be more melancholy than the contemplation of the remains of a meal), had set before me a small plate that appeared to be of silver, upon which, resting on an exquisite doily and fluctuating within their ample shells of mother-of-pearl, there lay in state six virgin oysters of a milky colour and of uncommon magnitude and purity.

"But I didn't order this !" I added with just resentment.

"Quite true, Sir," promptly rejoined the waiter with a grace worthy of such a gentleman, "but you must know," and here he lowered his voice, "that these oysters are extra and free of charge. To-day," and he lowered his voice to a whisper, "is St. Damian's."

"Yes ; but I have never heard that oysters have a patron saint, and of that name."

"No, Sir, not the oysters ! But the proprietor of the restaurant's son is called Damian : therefore to-day is his feast-day ; and it is our custom to offer on this occasion some delicacy to the worthy customers who honour us on a day which for his family is one of rejoicing."

What could one say to this ? I might have

raised doubts as to the veracity of the waiter's
assertion ; but upon lifting my eyes from the
costly plate and turning them towards the desk,
I saw that the distinguished youth who answered
to the happy name of Damian was already
looking at me and smiling profusely, as though
he meant to say : " Believe me, it is just as the
waiter has told you : you can eat them without
fear of contracting any debt or obligation ! "

What more could I want ?

I delicately took between my fingers one of
those precious molluscs, from which there eman-
ated a scent of sea-weed and of fresh ocean waves,
and swallowed it in one mouthful, " whose
sweetness," as the divine poet hath it, " still
lingers within me " (1) ; but—see the effect
of excessive libations !—I could not then remember this line properly.

The five remaining oysters suffered the same
fate as the first, and each one proved to be more
delicious than its predecessor.

" Greedy and clever Man," I thought to myself, " exploits earth, air and sea in order that he
may satisfy his appetites, and although the vice
of gluttony be despicable and unworthy of his
dignity, his frail nature certainly falls into it
more often than is beseeming." And those
oyster shells put me in mind of that beautiful

1. A reminiscence of Dante's eulogy on Casella's singing
(*Purgatorio*, canto 2nd, lines 113–114) : . . . *sì dolcemente,
che la dolcezza ancor dentro mi suona*, i.e. so sweetly, that the
sweetness thereof still resounds within me.

lyric of Zanella (1), entitled : " Upon a fossil shell," in which he says : " You wandered with shoals of nautili and murexes, when man was not." Never before had these lines seemed to me so full of mysterious significance !

The waiter removed the shells, and placed before me a fruit dish full of mandarins, dates and other rare and choice fruits of this earth, mother of all good and beautiful things. Now, I could not have said : " I refuse to have any fruit ! " for after such a lordly banquet, it would have been bad form.

Nevertheless, in the midst of my beatitude, I was struck by a bitter thought : that my day's wages as a schoolmaster would not be sufficient to pay for such a lavish feast. The total cost of all those dishes must certainly have exceeded the sum of which I can freely dispose each day, after twelve years in the teaching profession.

As this doubt was embittering the pleasant process of digestion, I decided to remove it. So I called the waiter.

" Yes, Sir ? "

" The bill, please ! "

He drew out from his dress coat his black, leather-bound cheque-book and brandished a formidable pencil (at that moment, the new bank-notes which I had just received at the Education Office lost some of their colour and paled).

1. A classicist poet of the Italian *Risorgimento*, author of the famous poem : *Sopra una conchiglia fossile*, from which Panzini here quotes lines 12–14.

" That's soon done, Sir : *table d'hôte* luncheon at two and a half *lire*, and "—here he just glanced at the flask out of the corner of his eye—" half a *lira* of wine ; three *lire* in all."

I breathed freely.

" You could not be more moderate ; I think I shall come here very often," I said, and this appreciation simply came out of its own accord.

" It is the policy of the firm, Sir," said that model Ganymede with simple modesty.

" Bring me some coffee, then."

" Will you take a small glass of cognac, as well ? "

" Why not ? Certainly : *semel in anno* (1).

But the praiseworthy waiter had gone, and when he returned with the vessels, he whispered in my ear :

" Would you like a contraband cigar ? I have some extra fine Havanas."

" It is illegal," said I.

" Oh, you needn't worry about that : the Attorney-General, who comes here to dine, smokes nothing but my Havanas ; in fact he has them in stock."

" If that is the case : *regis ad exemplum totus componitur orbis* (2)."

Whereupon this never-to-be-forgotten waiter lit me a Havana, whose light, bluish smoke,

1. A reference to the Latin saying : *semel in anno licet insanire*, i.e. once in the year it is allowable to act insanely.

2. *I.e.* the whole kingdom follows the example of the king.

mingling with the fogginess induced by the wine and by the liqueur, gently lulled me into a sense of infinite beatitude.

" The world is beautiful, and blessed is the future ! " (1) I repeated to myself with the great poet, " Yes, certainly, the world is beautiful " . . . and I no longer heard any sounds around me, although the hall was full of people.

When, behold ! Gradually, little by little, I became aware that the seat opposite to me was being moved ; I then opened my eyes, and saw that young Damian shyly sitting down before me.

" What does he want ? " I asked myself, opening my eyes still wider.

He was smiling, I could see that his florid face was smiling with pleasure and affection ; but then I heard these unkind words, which sadly disturbed my digestion :

" I see, Sir, that you do not recognise me. . . . But I know *you* very well ! "

" Alas ! " I sighed in my heart, " alas for the sweetness of my all too transient incognito ! "

" No, Sir, really, I have not the pleasure " . . . I faltered.

Still smiling, he went on :

" I was one of your pupils ten years ago ; but I can see that you do not remember my face, although I remember yours perfectly."

Again I sighed in my heart, and more deeply, for, being a highly sensitive man, I felt ashamed

1. A quotation from the 24th quatrain of G. Carducci's " Song of Love " (*Canto dell' amore*).

at being caught in the displeasing vice of gluttony
by one of my pupils.

Nevertheless, I answered :

" I am happy and grateful, indeed most grateful, that you should remember me ; but so many
youths have been pupils of mine, that I find it
very difficult to remember them individually."

" Oh, you must remember me very well,
though," he insisted, with a more enigmatic
smile.

" Believe me ! " . . . and I placed my hand
on my chest.

" My name is Damian Saltori—that ought to
recall something ! " He paused a moment, and
then uttered these terrible words :

" You ' plucked ' me inexorably at the ' pass '
examination from the third to the fourth *ginnasio* (1). Indeed you spoke of ' crushing ' and
not of ' plucking ' : see whether I remember or
not ? "

" What treachery is this ? " I thought to
myself, starting.

Farewell to my eupeptic siesta ! I do not
know what I answered ; but I certainly was
abashed, and I must have replied to this effect :

" I am sorry, I did not do it on purpose ! If
it really was so, I heartily regret it, I sincerely
do ! "

1. One of the courses of study open to pupils in the Italian
secondary schools. It lays special stress on languages, ancient
and modern, and literary subjects. It is akin to the German
Gymnasium, and is divided into five *classi* or stages.

" But I owe my life to you, Sir ! " the youth then exclaimed with the greatest enthusiasm and to my utmost astonishment. " My present prosperity, my good fortune, are entirely owing to you : how many times I would have liked to stop you in the street and express my gratitude ; only I had not the courage. But now that you have come into my place of business, I have taken the liberty " . . .

" Yes, but I don't understand " . . . I answered, still perturbed ; for I feared that my old pupil had remembered the figure of speech known by the name of ' irony.'

" Oh, it's quite clear : it's as clear as daylight. Do you remember what you used to say to me ? "

" I ? No, I don't ! "

" You used to say : ' You are a thoroughly good boy ; but in order to follow a course of classical studies, something more than mere intelligence is required (and you do not possess even this) : one requires an artistic sense. Now you have no artistic sense : you are an oyster.' Oh, I remember it well, you know ! "

I blushed at the memory of the exquisite oysters which I had recently devoured, and I felt as though they were all still alive and in their shells within me.

" I am very sorry, really " . . . I said, in the height of my embarrassment.

" Why, not at all, you were telling a Gospel truth," continued the excellent Damian. " It was my parents who would not understand : I had

at all costs to become a lawyer, to ennoble the
family with the title of Doctor, and therefore I
even had tutors to give me private lessons ! But
I could not swallow the Latin, and those Italian
compositions gave me cold perspiration. You
failed me, and you did quite right."

" I do not remember " . . .

" Don't you remember, Sir, that scene between
you and my father ? And that M.P., a customer
of ours, who demanded my examination papers
from the Principal, that he might take them to the
Ministry of Education ? And the threat to
demand an official provision ? "

Then I did indeed remember ; it was the
Hon. ——, but I had better not give his name.

" But you held out," continued the amiable
Damian. " They wanted to stretch two fours
until they became two sixes (1), but you would
not hear of it ; even the Principal wanted to
stretch the two fours, but you would not !
And my father said (it makes me laugh when I
think of it) : ' What ? I allow my debtors
discounts of hundreds of *lire*, and you make all
this fuss for one or two marks ! ' "

" Well, you see " . . .

" But you did just the right thing ! After that,
my parents understood. They sent me, as I
desired, to Switzerland, where I learnt modern
languages and received a commercial education.
I wanted to go on enlarging my father's business,

1. In Italian scholastic examinations, all candidates must
obtain a minimum of six marks out of ten in order to pass.

while he wanted to retire. . . . Now, at any
rate, I am very prosperous. I could not stand
that Cornelius Nepos " . . .

" You were quite right ! "

And he himself helped me to put on my overcoat ; he then handed me my hat and stick, and
begged me to come often and honour his place.

" I shall never forget St. Damian's day," I said.

" It is very kind of you to say so, Sir ! "

And he himself held the door open, while I
emerged from the restaurant with that superb
Havana between my lips, like a banker or a
nobleman who certainly does not limit his
expenditure at lunch.

From *Piccole storie del Mondo grande*,
Fratelli Treves, Milano, 1901.

PAPINI

Giovanni Papini was born at Florence in
1881. He left school before he was fifteen, and
never attended a college or a university.

Delicate in health from early childhood, he
soon showed remarkable intellectual powers,
which developed in him with extraordinary
precocity. As a boy, he was distinguished by
that morbid misanthropy and love for solitude
which are so vividly portrayed in the first chapter
of *Un uomo finito*.

In 1903 he founded the review *Leonardo*, and
was its director until it came to an end in 1907 ;
he contributed largely to the *Voce* and for a time
(1912) directed it ; together with Amendola he
directed the *Anima* (1911), and in 1913, in
conjunction with Soffici, he founded *Lacerba*,
a review which lasted until 1915.

He married in 1907, and since then he has
been living partly in Florence and partly at
Bulciano, in the higher valley of the Tiber.

His principal works, in order of publication,
are : *Il tragico quotidiano* (1906), *Il crepuscolo dei
filosofi* (1907), *Il pilota cieco* (1907), *Memorie
d'Iddio* (1911), *Vita di nessuno* (1912), *Parole e
sangue* (1912), *24 cervelli* (1912), *Un uomo
finito* (1912), *Pragmatismo* (1913), *Buffonate*
(1914), *Maschilità* (1915), *Cento pagine di poesia*
(1915), *La paga del sabato* (1915), *Stroncature*
(1916), *L'opera prima* (1917), *L'uomo Carducci*
(1918), *Testimonianze* (1918), *Polemiche religiose*

(1918), *Giorni di festa* (1918), *L'esperienza futurista* (1919), *Storia di Cristo* (1921), *Pane e vino* (1926), *Sant' Agostino* (1929). In collaboration with Domenico Giuliotti he has published the *Dizionario dell' Omo Salvatico* (1923).

A HALF-PORTRAIT

I HAVE never been a child. I had no childhood.

Fair, warm days of childish exhilaration ; the long tranquillity of innocence ; surprises in the daily discovery of the universe : what are they ?

I do not know them, or I do not remember them.

I knew of them from books, afterwards ; and now I divine them in the boys that I meet. But I felt and experienced them in myself for the first time only after I had passed my twentieth year, in some happy moments of respite or self-forgetfulness.

Childhood means love, joy, *insouciance* ; and I see myself, in the past, *always* alone and thoughtful.

From a child, I have felt tremendously solitary and different—I do not know why. Was it perhaps because my people were poor, or because I was born different from others ?—I cannot say. I only remember that when I was six or seven years old, a young aunt of mine gave me the nickname of *old-man*, and that all my relations accepted it. And in fact I was, for the most part, serious and gloomy : I talked little, even with other boys ; forms of politeness annoyed me ; suave affectations irritated me ; and to the unbridled riot of my companions in their happiest years, I preferred the solitude of the most sheltered corners of our poor, dark, little house. I was, in short, what the ladies who wear hats call a ' contrary child,' and the women who go without, a ' toad.' They were right : I was, I must have been, tremendously disliked by everybody. And I remember that I felt very keenly this dislike in those around me, and it made me more timid, more melancholy and more morose than ever.

When, by chance, I found myself with other boys, I hardly ever entered into their games. I liked to remain apart, regarding them with my serious, green eyes : the eyes of a critic and of an enemy. Not because I envied them : it was contempt rather which I felt within me at such moments.

From that time began the war between me and mankind. I avoided them, and they neglected me ; I did not love them, and they hated me. Out of doors, in the public gardens, some would drive me away and others would laugh behind my back ; at school, they pulled my curls or complained of me to the masters ; in the country, even when I was on my grandfather's land, the country boys threw stones at me, without my having done anything to anybody—almost as though they felt me to be of another race.

My relations invited me or caressed me only
when they could not help doing so, in order not
to show a too indecent partiality before other
people ; but I was very well aware of this
pretence, and hid myself, replying rudely and
sharply to every word they said.

One memory more than all others remains
engraved upon my heart : wet Sunday evenings
of November or December in my grandfather's
house, with the bowl of warmed wine in the centre
of the table, just under the large, bronzed oil
lamp, with the platter of roasted chestnuts beside
it, and all the family—uncles and aunts and
cousins in quantity, and of both sexes—with their
flushed faces around it.

Near the fire, the patriarch, white and witty,
laughed and drank.   The logs crackled, already
half-covered with delicate ashes ;   the glasses
rattled on the plates ;   the bigoted and knowing
aunts cackled about the happenings and scandals
of the week ;   and the children laughed and
shrieked in the midst of the blue smoke of their
fathers' cigars.   As for me, the buzz of this
cheap and senseless merry-making made both my
head and my soul ache.   I felt myself a stranger
there: very far indeed from them all.   And as
soon as I could, I slipped out unnoticed through
the door, and with careful steps, brushing along
the damp wall, I turned into the long, dark
passage which led to the front door of the house.
And there I felt my little, solitary heart beat
violently, just as if I had been about to do I do

not know what evil deed, to commit an act of treachery.

In that passage there was a glass door which opened out into a small uncovered court : I used to open it a very little, and start listening to the rain which fell wearily and reluctantly, splashing on to the tiles and into the pools, rain which fell without enthusiasm, without fury, but with the slow and hateful obstinacy of something that will never stop. And I used to stay in the dark listening to it, with the cold air on my face and with tears in my eyes, and if through the slightly open door an occasional drop suddenly splashed on to my skin, I felt happy, as though it had come to purify me and to invite me elsewhere, to somewhere beyond houses and Sundays. But then a voice would call me back to the light, to torture and to remarks : " What a badly-behaved child ! "

Yes, it is true : I have never been a child. I have always been an ' old-man ' and a ' toad,' thoughtful and gloomy. Even in those days the best part of my life was lived within me. Even then, shut out from all joy and affection, I retired into myself, I expanded inwardly in eager imaginings and in solitary ruminations upon a world reshaped through my own *ego*.

I was not pleasing to others, and their aversion confined me to solitude. Solitude made me even sadder and yet more displeasing ; and this sadness locked up my heart and spurred my brain. My being so different severed me even from those who were near to me, and this separation made me yet more different. Thus from the very beginning of life, I began to taste the virile sweetness of that infinite and indefinite melancholy which seeks not for distraction nor for consolation, but aimlessly consumes itself within, creating little by little that habit of living internally and alone, which withdraws us for ever from our kind.

No, I have never experienced childhood. I do not remember in the least ever having been a child. I always visualise myself in the past as brooding and intractable, silent and apart, without a smile or a single outburst of frank pleasure. I see myself always pale and wondering, as in my first portrait.

The photograph is torn in half, just under the heart. It is small, dirty and discoloured: and the borders of the little card are black, like those used for mourning. The blanched face of an abstracted child gazes towards the left, but one feels that there, on the left, regarding him, there is nobody. The eyes are sad and rather sunken —was it because they did not come out well ?— the mouth is forcibly closed and the lips slightly compressed, in order not to show the teeth. The one and only beauty is the long, soft curls which fall in rings on to the collar of the sailor-suit.

My mother says it is I, at seven years of age. It may be. This portrait is the one proof that I possess of my childhood. But does this seem to you the likeness of a child ? This little washed-out spectre that does not look at me, that does not want to look at anybody ?

One can see immediately that those eyes are not made to be tinted with Heaven's blue : they are grey, and clouded in themselves. One can divine that those cheeks are white and wan, and that they always will be so : they will redden only through fatigue or shame. And those lips so tightly, so voluntarily closed, are not made to open in laughter, in speech, in prayer, or to utter a cry. They are the closed lips of one who will suffer without the tiresome weakness of complaint. They are lips that will be kissed too late.

In this faded half of a photograph, I rediscover the dead soul of those days : the delicate face of the ' toad,' the frown of the ' contrary child,' and the quiet sadness of the ' old-man.' And it goes to my heart to think of all those dreary days and endless years, of that imprisoned life, of that sadness without cause, of that ineradicable nostalgia for other skies and other companions.

No, no : that is not the portrait of a child. I tell you again, I have had no childhood.

> *Un uomo finito*, chapter 1. Vallecchi,
> Firenze, 1925. (By kind permission
> of the author and of Messrs. Hodder
> & Stoughton, Ltd.)

THE DISCOVERY OF EVIL

FROM an unsociable and precociously intro-
spective childhood ; from a humiliating
solitude imposed upon me by timidity, by
difference and by poverty ; from the repeated
defeats of aims too ambitiously encyclopædic ;
from elegiac lyricism ruminated along grey
streets, between blackened walls and under ashen
skies ; from confused impulses towards a worthy,
heroic and poetic existence, immediately frus-
trated and drowned in the detestable daily round
of a restricted, provincial, stinted and mortifying
life ; there resulted a hopeless pessimism, locked
up in itself, like a fortress without windows.
As soon as the intellect—at the close of my
adolescence—came of age, it asked of life its
purpose, and received no answer. Then theory
gave to melancholy a form. The absolute
physical gloom of those festive gatherings on
winter evenings (1) was followed by an enquiry
into the benefits and evils of existence, and the
mind answered *no* to every promise, it replied
no to every lying dream, and blew over my last
magical illusions like the midnight wind over the
few remaining lights of a waning illumination.

The languor of fantasticating vigils, when the
desire comes to pity oneself without any reason,
as one will never pity anyone else, was followed
by enquiries into the nature of pain, into the

1. See the preceding chapter : " A half-portrait."

brevity of joy and into the balance of earthly happiness ; the pathetic sonnets on the decline of the day or on the end of Autumn were succeeded by a firm intention to protest publicly and rationally against the brutish acceptance of life.

At that age, there presented itself to me again and again in the unchanging words of all times and of all the weary, the eternal, useless question: Is life worth living ?

What answer could I give ? Life promised me little, and gave me nothing. I could not expect riches, nor triumphs in learning, because from the outset I had of necessity entered upon a brief and mediocre course of scholastic studies, nor love of women, because I was both ugly and timid, nor boundless knowledge, because I could not bear to think of unfinished enterprises. Few troubled themselves about me—no one was fond of me, beyond my father and mother, who were too far away from this soul that had indeed sprung from theirs, but which, even to them, seemed an alien one.

Nothing remained to me but thought : I had always liked to generalise, to establish connections between distant facts, to divine laws, to take theories to pieces and to build them up again. Not long before this time, fresh from the study of the ' New Science ' (1), which I had not properly understood, I conceived the idea of constructing a philosophy of the history of literature, and I

1. An allusion to G. B. Vico's *Principi della Scienza Nuova.*

fancied that I had discovered the reasons for the ebb and flow of art, and the causes of the greatness and decay of literatures. It was then that Taine widened my mind and made me envy his facility in drawing clear schemata of well-ordered and symmetrical ideas, barely coloured between one line and another by handfuls of facts : the demon of speculation was already lying in wait for the youthful poet, and cramming him with formulæ, maxims and well-deduced corollaries.

Thus thought, already armed, flung itself upon this miserable life, so devoid of all joy and brightness, and soon discovered its emptiness and its pent-up suffering. Is this all that it comes to then ? To every longing a repulse, to every aspiration a denial, at every effort only a rebuff— to all the desire for happiness which comes to us at sixteen, at eighteen, only the promise of nothing ? Nothingness disguised in a hundred different ways ! Faith, glory, art, action, paradise, conquest : masks without faces, sockets without eyes, mouths without tongues, and kisses without response.

Life, to be bearable, must be lived intensely. Our sensibilities fill it from moment to moment, and even if it be mutable as running water, at least it carries us along as on a current which may seem constant and eternal. But if life be analysed, stripped and laid bare by thought, reason, logic and philosophy, then the void is seen to be abysmal, nothingness frankly confesses itself to be nothingness, and despair settles on the

soul as the angel rested on the deserted sepulchre
of the Son of God.

Thus it happened that with all the ardour
of a growing life I became confirmed in the
negation of life. My reply—the only one then
possible—to the malign injustice of fate and
the silent enmity of mankind, was my conviction
of the infinite vanity of all things, of the inborn
baseness and ineradicable wretchedness of the
human species. But my pessimism, however
much I proclaimed and believed it to be deeply
rooted, was not consistent and did not go as far
as it might and ought to have done. At first,
it was merely poetic and literary. The rabid
encyclopædist and the budding lyrist that were
within me divided the task between them.
Even the discovery of the infelicity of life was a
pretext for new compilations. In my readings,
I gathered together all the effusions of the poets,
the sallies of the dramatists, the points of the
orators, the admonishments of the preachers
and the aphorisms of the dabblers and adepts
in philosophy in which, explicitly or implicitly,
there was shown or lamented the uselessness of
existence, the prevalence of evil, the sadness of
unfulfilled dreams and of torn illusions, sorrow
for the irrecoverable past, and that despair
which bends and breaks the soul after one has
circumnavigated life—a narrow, dimly lighted
island in the infinite whirlpool of nothingness.
I thus compiled a funereal medley of affliction
put into words, in which the couplets, the para-

doxes, the laments and the regrets, of men far
removed from each other in space, in time and
in spirit, were to be found jumbled together as
in an anguished chorus of human discontent.

This I did not merely out of literary curiosity,
for I was sincere in my pessimism. To find
others thus cursing and disconsolate gave me
heart. It seemed to me that I was no longer
alone, that I had found my brothers, my born
companions, and my consolers among the dead.
It appeared to me that I could not be wrong in
my negation of life, that it was not merely the
cowardly protest of a boy spoilt by disorderly
dreaming. But I did not confine myself to
making a patchwork of wise maxims : I myself
thought of writing a book, the true book on life,
the book which was to persuade every man once
and for all to regard himself and others, and in
fact the whole of existence, with the contempt
which it deserves.

Just then, I came in contact for the first time
with a great philosopher. I dipped into, read
and meditated upon Schopenhauer, in bits, in
pieces, and at intervals, but sufficiently to feel
that the facile science of my little manuals of
geology or of evolutionism was not the highest
point attainable by our cognitive intelligence.

I then attempted to trace a history of pessimism,
and in that way traversed with great strides the
whole history of philosophy, wherein other ideas,
besides the negative and painful ones, attracted
me and aroused my curiosity. The scholar was

no longer alone : the theorist was growing and
strengthening himself. The ordering of my
system of pessimistic philosophy—founded on
the law that the most desirable ends are precisely
those that are necessarily unattainable—was
accompanied by intellectual joys that were
almost new to me. Nor did I fail to be carried
to outremos and to arrive at sweeping conclusions.

Schopenhauer's hostility to suicide displeased
me ; I, on the contrary, elaborated, as the
concluding part of my great work, a stoical
advocacy of universal suicide. This was not
mere sensationalism : I saw no other solution.
I did not mean individual suicide : that being
both ridiculous and useless, but a suicide *en
masse*, a conscientious and concordantly deliber-
ated suicide, such as would leave the earth alone
and deserted to revolve uselessly in the heavens.

I fancied I could found a society which would
grow little by little, and spread together with
the diffusion of my irrefutable book ; and when
this league of despairing men had at last em-
braced the whole of mankind, then the great
day would have to be chosen : the day for the
end !

I had even thought out the means, and it
seemed to me that poison was undoubtedly the
one to be preferred.

Folly ! Childishness ! All the same, the
fixed idea of my destination to be the apostle
of this supreme conclusion to human life was
for me, at a certain time, the one and only pretext

for remaining alive. I consented to live, only
in the absurd hope of making all men die
together with me.

> *Un uomo finito*, chapter 8. Vallecchi,
> Firenze, 1925. (By kind permission
> of the author and of Messrs. Hodder
> & Stoughton, Ltd.)

SOFFICI

ARDENGO SOFFICI was born in 1879 at Rignano, on the Arno. He left school at an early age and studied privately.

His interest in the plastic arts, and especially in painting, took him to Paris, where he lived more or less continuously from 1900 to 1907. On his return to Florence, he joined the *Voce* group and organised the first exhibition of French impressionist art in Italy. In 1913 he allied himself with the futurists, and in conjunction with Papini founded the review *Lacerba*. During the War, he was wounded twice, and his soldiering experiences were embodied in *Kobilek* (1918). He now lives at the Fornaci, near Florence. Since 1925, he has been a regular contributor to the *Selvaggio*, a Fascist literary review.

His principal works, in order of publication, are : *Ignoto toscano* (1909), *Il Caso Rosso e l'impressionismo* (1909), *Arthur Rimbaud* (1911), *Lemmonio Boreo* (1912), *Cubismo e oltre* (1913), *Arlecchino* (1914), *Giornale di bordo* (1915), *Bïf § zf + 18. Simultaneità. Chimismi lirici* (1915), *Kobilek* (1918), *La giostra dei sensi* (1919), *La ritirata del Friuli* (1919), *Scoperte e massacri* (1919), *Statue e fantocci* (1919), *Rete mediterranea* (1920), *Principi di Estetica Futurista* (1922), *Battaglia fra due vittorie* (1923), *L'elegia dell' Ambra* (1927), *Medardo Rosso* (1929), *Periplo dell' Arte* (1929).

THE LOG-BOOK

April 14*th.*

I HAVE gathered a spray of orange-coloured wallflowers, a little bunch of periwinkles and three wild hyacinths of a dark indigo blue, which I like to keep in a glass of water on the table, while I am having my meals. I love to gaze at their transparent petals against the window, to contemplate the flower bells over-flowing with light, to admire the sunlight as it plays with the colours and reflections of the flowers and of the water ; I love to smell, together with the odours of warm bread, of various dishes and of fruits, a little of the per-fume of Spring that is scattered throughout the country.

My mother, who is a fervent Christian, regards these flowers with indifference, almost with aversion, as a superfluous pleasure ; and in her eyes I can perceive a faint shadow of reproof every time she hastens to remove them in order to clear the table.

Years ago, in Paris, I knew a charlatan from Bari, one who affected paganism and theosophy, who, if in lighting my cigarette I admired the red and bluish flame of the match, or contem-plated the moon through the flowering branches of the horse chestnuts on the boulevard, would explain to me the mystic meaning of the Pyramids, symbolic representations of ascending fire, and the influence exercised by the planets over the astral body, or the profound hieratic significance of the myth of Diana.

Well, it is largely for such trifling motives (Oh, what frivolity !) that I hate religions : religions which despise the simple pleasures of the senses, or congeal with their vain cabals and reasonings the living and enchanting phenomena of the universe.

THE TWO ARTICHOKES

April 16th.

I DO not intend to be unduly partial towards my own country ; I only want to consider the great difference there is between these two artichokes, which the maid brought in this morning.

They are very different : one comes from Naples, and the other from Empoli.

The Neapolitan is bright-coloured, round and as free from superfluous leaves as a beautiful rose ; it is jovial and full of promising magnificence. One might liken it to the plump face of a good-natured squire, all cordiality and laden with riches which any friend could enjoy without ceremony—an ideal artichoke.

The other one, the Tuscan, is a monster in comparison. It is lean, rough-skinned, livid, and looks like a wild thistle. Its long and

narrow leaves are drawn close together like
uncouth, sordid country-folk, who are ashamed
of themselves or afraid of being cheated out of
a centime—and, each one bears a thorn which
you dare not touch.

This artichoke is a living image of barrenness
and intractability.

Let us try plucking off their leaves, though.

I tear away the outermost scales from the
Southerner, and I find others, fairer and more
tender—but really rather stringy and tasteless.
Patience ! There are many of them and the
good ones are bound to be sufficiently plentiful.
So, I keep on peeling off.

The third layer is even more handsome than
the second, and the fifth one is more showy than
the fourth, and so on—but they are always
tasteless, however. It doesn't matter ; let us
go on peeling and peeling. And indeed, look !
we have come at last to something worth having:
but the leaves are already getting smaller,
thinner, more flabby and dispirited. . . .

At the tenth layer, we find them reduced to
mere petals of withering choke-weed. I now
pluck these away also and—the devil !—I find
a colourless hollow surrounded by vain, worth-
less hairs.

But, in the Tuscan, we find that even the
fleshy bases of the outer leaves are rich and tasty.
Almost half the next layer is eatable, the third
and fourth strata are delicious, and the more we
advance towards the centre, the more complete

does our gluttonous joy become. Then, what shall I say of the centre, the heart ? of that little compact morsel, pure, amber-coloured, tender and creaking, in which are concentrated all the tastes, perfumes and freshness of Spring ?

Again I say that I do not want to show any partiality or make any literary or philosophical allusions ; but does it not seem, even to you, that these two artichokes, this contrast, these appearances and these substances, might suggest comparisons . . . comparisons . . . how shall I put it ? . . . of a higher order ?

A STORM

July 23rd.

IT has been preparing itself since yesterday evening. All night long there has been distant thunder and lightning, followed by gusts of wind.

Now it is breaking. The sky, which had exhibited at its horizon a kind of bright sulphureous rent and from which not long ago there hung enormous ashen clouds, with the frayed and dangling edges of outstretched rags, is now all closed, grey, yellowish and uniform.

Every second there comes a palpitating flash of a violet or greenish hue, immediately followed by a formidable clap of thunder which makes the panes of my window to resound and then, rumbling itself away to infinity, rolls through the still darker atmosphere towards the West until another more distant clap smothers its last reverberations. The rain pelts down furiously, forming a closely knit rigging ; the wind drives it sideways, and then its strings are like glass arrows shot obliquely from above. The trees writhe beneath the whirling wind.

There is a certain anguish in the movements of the tree tops and of the vine branches, whose sprigs seem like poor animals chained to or half buried in the earth, which are trying to free themselves and escape. Meanwhile the rain strikes them, washes them and makes their leaves shine. The horizon of the fields is lost in a dense, blind fog, which would appear to be the sky descending upon the earth in the form of a cataract, and only a few hundred yards away.

But see, the storm is relenting. The thunder and lightning still continue, but the air is a little clearer ; the rain falls calmly and regularly. Now the plants are only barely waving, as though resigned or even pleased with this humidity after so much burning heat, with this fresh rain which waters them and drenches the ground into which they bury their roots.

The road has taken on a sombre colour, and the overflowing rivulet that runs along by the hedge is thick and yellow, like cream.

And I am surprised to find myself all washed, refreshed and restored, just as much as the road and the trees.

From *Giornale di Bordo*. (Libreria della ' Voce,' Firenze, 1915.)

THE TOUR

THE last greenness of a season which no longer appears to desire existence, save through the cunning art of lyrical pictures, is allying itself to the greyness of the sky and of all things in order to create a circular, *finis vitae* dome of silence, which is only just broken by the twitter of a quivering robin red-breast on the pointed branch of a cornel tree.

Silent are the bugles of a war-like hope proclaiming, between one victory and another, riches and greatness of all kinds, glories of an existence such as books, heroes and a too ardent enthusiasm had promised us.

Amidst the hedges, another joy is, instead, open to us : that of disappearing in so far as our bodily and mental organism is concerned and melting away, as an autonomous sensuousness, into the phenomena of pure music and light.

All wisdom and perfect bliss now lie in adhering to the logic of the soil, to the logic of the silent grass in yonder running, winding water, which reflects patches of blue sky ; in receiving, more delicately than a lily, the impressions of the wind, the hieroglyphics of song.

Our will is now but a remembrance of past time—we are quite content if only our feet will consent to walk through the landscape, to make a tour of all these marvels. Only the senses now remain active, as in the primeval ages, when we bathed in colours, in sounds, in perfumes, and in the elemental love of the early Scriptures.

The red house of the peasant causes us more astonishment than we would experience if we saw a rigidly geometrical flower growing on the summit of a hill. Yet the tall chimney waves its industrial banner of smoke without gainsaying the formula of the landscape, and the poor salute this mystery as though they had nothing to ask from the majesty of the world.

Were it not for a curious deficiency of voice, one might sing :

> With these autumn leaves,
> There are bushels of gold throughout the country.

or :

> How contented are the plants,
> All drenched with the cold rain !
> And I am as drenched with happiness
> As the humid plants of the gardens.

But we prefer to melt away.

What conveys a rather sinister impression is the whirring of a flight of sparrows.

We now feel as though we would stagnate, with a taste of ashes and of obscurity, in the stone urn overgrown with moss which stands erect upon the column alongside the old gate of the manor.

The tour has been accomplished. If we went any further, we should find nothingness.

From *Bif* § *zf* + 18. *Simultaneità. Chimismi lirici.* (La 'Voce,' Firenze, 1915.)

OJETTI

Ugo Ojetti was born at Rome in 1871. As a journalist, his productiveness has been continuous from 1894, when he began by contributing to Attilio Luzzatto's *Tribuna* and to Luigi Lodi's *Nuova Rassegna*. Since 1898, he has been a regular contributor to the *Corriere della Sera*. He has travelled extensively in Europe, in Egypt, in Central Asia and in the United States. He has been a prominent organiser of art exhibitions in Italy and, like Soffici, an art critic of outstanding merit. In 1920 he founded the review of fine arts *Dedalo*, of which he is still the director, and in 1929 *Pegaso*, a literary review.

His principal literary works, in order of publication, are : *Senza Dio* (1893), *Alla scoperta dei letterati* (1894), *Il vecchio* (1898), *L'onesta viltà* (1898), *Il gioco dell' amore* (1900), *Le vie del peccato* (1902), *Il Cavallo di Troia* (1904), *Mimì e la gloria* (1906), *I capricci del conte Ottavio* (1907–1909), *Ritratti d'artisti italiani* (1911–1923), *Donne, uomini e burattini* (1912), *L'amore e suo figlio* (1913), *I nani tra le colonne* (1920), *Raffaello e altre leggi* (1921), *Confidenze di pazzi e di savii sui tempi che corrono* (1921), *Mio figlio ferroviere* (1922), *Cose viste* (1923–1926), *Scrittori che si confessano* (1926), *Il ritratto italiano dal 1500 al 1800* (1927), *Tintoretto, Canova, Fattori* (1928), *U. Foscolo* (1928), *La pittura italiana nell' Ottocento* (1928), *Bello e Brutto* (1930).

EINSTEIN'S FACE

BOLOGNA, *October 26th*, 1921.

WITH his theory of relativity, Professor Einstein wishes to appeal only to the minds of physicists and mathematicians. But if he had felt to-day the desire, which comes sometimes to every discoverer, for an excursion outside his own field, he would have found the most beautiful of relativities here in the hall of the Archiginnasio (1), just a little above his head. On the wall behind him, we listeners, although endeavouring to be as attentive as possible, could not but notice that close to the ceiling there was a painting of a large, queenly Madonna and Child, and that below the Madonna there was a bust, probably in marble, of Victor Emanuel II, and finally, that below the bust there was Einstein, a plump, alert and smiling Jew, who was speaking to us more or less about paradise, at least about the place where Dante imagined it to be : in the sky and among the stars. Our Italian history abounds in these peaceful combinations of many relativities : that is why it is so beautiful. Certainly Einstein had never as yet spoken under the protection of the Madonna. His beautiful, pale, Semitic face has a yellowish hue which, at least at a distance and against the dark background of a blackboard, makes it appear more swollen

1. The University of Bologna ; so called because it is the oldest in Europe.

than fat. He has curly and glossy black hair, with just a touch of silver ; his lips, beneath a small black moustache, are full and rosy ; his eyes are round, with short, high eyebrows, which are far apart, so that when he raises his eyes in search of a word his whole face assumes a fascinating air of stupefaction and almost of ecstasy. But what wins the heart is his childlike expression : he is a great, serene and well-mannered child, happy to play, as he does, with ideas, with worlds and with infinity. His fat, soft, shiny hands, issuing from sleeves that are too short and too narrow, his timid and restricted gestures, his slow, lisping and uncertain delivery, his sincere, jovial and ready smile, increase this sweet and childlike impression ; and does he not tell us his theory as gracefully as one tells a fairy-tale, and with the child's faith in fairy-tales ? " There were seven stars, thus " . . . and on the blackboard he marked the seven white stars, and then a circle, the sun. " The world is infinite, but it is limited " . . . and he smiled as though, in playing, he had thrown the ball so high that even he could no longer see it.

This childlike serenity and freshness is the charm by which he holds his great audiences captive and, as they say, ' enamoured.' It is this quality in him which makes us feel the affinity between this inexorable mathematician, whose name suggests the hardness of stone, and a poet. He has the same wings, the same thirst for infinity, the same faith in the reality of dreams, that is to say of hypotheses : the same faith in the absoluteness of even the relative. The Christian Madonna on her throne, which is eternal, I know, but which is here painted, and therefore transitory and relative, seemed to look down upon him with benevolence.

MUSSOLINI SPEAKS

Rome, *November 8th*, 1921.

AT the *Augusteo*, from the press gallery. I had never heard a speech by Mussolini. He stood out against the red velvet curtain that hangs over the stage. He has two faces in one : the upper face, from the nose upwards, and the lower face, mouth, chin and jaw. Between them there is no logical connection : sometimes, by tightening his jaw, by protruding his chin and contracting his eyebrows, Mussolini succeeds in imposing a connection between his two half-faces, in conciliating them for a moment through an effort of will. The round eyes, which are near together, the bare and open forehead, the short and quivering nose—these constitute his mobile and romantic ·countenance ; the other countenance, straight lips, prominent jaw and square chin, is his fixed, voluntary and one might say classical pose. When he raises his eyebrows, they form an acute angle above his nose, which reminds one of the sarcastic and tragic masks of Japan. When, on the other hand, he frowns, they form a clear horizontal line and his eyes disappear beneath two dark arches, and between that bare forehead and that square chin there appears a gloomy and rigid mask, which may well be called Napoleonic. Which is the real countenance of Benito Mussolini?

An extremely practised orator, master of himself, always before the public, he comments on each sentence and with an appropriate expression of his face. His gestures are restrained. He often uses his right hand only, keeping the left in his pocket and his left arm close to his side. Occasionally he puts both hands in his pockets : this is the statuesque moment of recapitulation, the *finale*. During the rare moments in which this restrained figure of an orator opens and frees itself, the two arms revolve high above the head, the ten fingers move as though they were seeking in the air for chords to strike, and the words precipitate as in a cataract. Just for a moment ; then Mussolini again becomes still and gloomy, and with two fingers feels the bow of his elegant tie in order to make sure that it is quite straight. These moments of tumultuous gesticulation are not the stirring moments ; they are generally the conclusion of a logical demonstration, a way of representing to the public the multitude of other reasons which he enumerates, indicates or omits for the sake of brevity : a kind of mimetic *etcetera*, which is extremely effective.

But besides the mimetics of a fine speaker, Mussolini has three other qualities by which he conquers his audience. The first is a well-rounded phraseology, which never cuts short a single sentence. The second is a frequency of picturesque and incisive definitions of a moral character, as, for instance, against the particularists : " The Italians, it seems, are already tired of being Italians " ; in praise of the forerunners of Fascism : " But for the Fascists of 1919 and 1920, the unknown soldier would not be resting to-day on the Capitol " ; and against the advocates of violence : "You must cure yourselves of my faults." The third quality is a continual, decisive, tranquillising affirmation, on which most people can trustfully rest : no mist, no uncertain colours, the whole world reduced to black and white. His doubts he keeps to himself.

The speech is drawing to a close. His face, through fatigue, has become leaner, more bony, more rigid.

As soon as he has finished and is moving towards the steps to descend, the Hon. Capanni seizes him by the waist and raises him above the crowd, with the gesture of the priest who raises the pyx containing the Consecrated Host. Beside me there are two boys in black shirts who have tears in their eyes. If Mussolini could see these tears, he would be more proud of them than of any applause.

PIRANDELLO AS AN ANCIENT CHINAMAN

FLORENCE, *December 17th*, 1922.

I HAVE found a noble counterpart to Luigi Pirandello. He resembles Lâo-tsze. Lâo-tsze was a Chinese philosopher, who lived about twenty-five centuries ago. I do not know how Adriano Tilgher (1), who is also a philosopher and often a Chinese one, will welcome this resemblance of his beloved Pirandello. But there it is: Pirandello resembles Lâo-tsze, and therefore Lâo-tsze resembles Pirandello.

I must confess that when I made this discovery, the light was dim. Pirandello and I were seated side by side in the pit of the *Politeama Nazionale* at Florence ; this was during the final rehearsal of " Clothing the Naked." The auditorium of that theatre is the barest in Italy : a vaulting which visibly consists of tiles and rafters ; chairs instead of stalls, chairs with white seats of coarse plaited straw like those one finds in a church. Only the seat on which Pirandello was sitting had a cushion, and this was rose-coloured, but faded and hard as became a cruel and sceptical author. A naked auditorium for " Naked life," " Naked masks," etc., plays by L. Pirandello.

We were alone in the pit. Pirandello was

1. Adriano Tilgher, a contemporary Italian critic, who has made a special study of Pirandello's works and ideas.

resting both hands on the knob of his stick and leaning forward towards the lighted stage and towards his characters. He was smiling. He was smiling and content because the actors satisfied him ; because the empty intrigues of his heroine, which were to make for herself a pretty dress of lies, if only to die in, emerged clearly from the good acting ; and moreover, because his comedy pleased him (and he was quite justified). In smiling he half closed his eyes, raised his eyebrows and stroked his little pointed white beard——

The Chinaman Lâo-tsze, the living image of him ! The same smile, the same eyes, the same cheek bones, the same mouth and beard, the same baldness and the same resigned goodness or at least the same sly resignation. Lâo-tsze, in truth, I have only known in bronze, in the many large and small bronze statues which represent him as sitting on a buffalo in the act, even in such a place, of writing and smiling. But apart from the buffalo, which can always be explained as a symbol (spontaneous life, criticism, or the Authors' Guild, etc.), the resemblance was marvellous. Lâo-tsze was so wise that when he was born his hair and eyebrows were already white ; and it was the same with Pirandello, at least in his capacity of playwright, for he began his dramatic career when he was almost fifty. Lâo-tsze was extremely learned, the librarian of a prince belonging to the Châu dynasty ; and Pirandello is a professor. 'Professor ' . . . ' Professor'—everyone, from the leading actress to the humblest clerk, calls him by this title, which had hitherto never been used on the stage. But this is nothing ; this is only on the surface. If we enter into the mind of Lâo-tsze, the resemblance becomes still closer. What, for Lâo-tsze, was this earth which we prize so dearly ! The bedlam of the universe. All kinds of madness fall from all parts of the cosmos on to the earth, as towards their proper centre of gravity.

A man belonging to the state of Tsin had a most healthy son who, when fully grown, began to feel and to think contrarily to most people : to him white was black, and sweetness was bitterness, perfume stench, honesty dishonesty and joy extreme sadness. His perturbed father told all this to Lâo-tsze, and Lâo-tsze answered solemnly : " And do you think him mad on that account ? Everyone suffers from the same distemper ; your son's malady is but a common one. Nor would it be so great a calamity were there only one madman in each family or a family of madmen in each village or a village of madmen in each town. But the whole world is nothing but a cage full of madmen. Even I am not quite sure whether my mind is properly balanced."

Of course, here Lâo-tsze—Pirandello was exaggerating through his love of logic. But think what a fine subject this would be for a comedy : Lâo-tsze, after twenty-five centuries, assumes the form of Pirandello. Pirandello discovers that he is Lâo-tsze and wants to become Pirandello again.   Lâo-tsze finds himself very much at home in Pirandello and does not wish to depart.   Finally Pirandello and Lâo-tsze agree to separate for one act only ; but when they are on the point of separation, their ideas (which would be so many distinct characters) no longer know which of them belong to Pirandello and which to Lâo-tsze.   Then these afflicted ideas enter into a third character, which is Pirandello *and* Lâo-tsze, but no longer either Pirandello or Lâo-tsze. . . .

Excuse me, Tilgher, but would you mind going on ?

From *Cose Viste, primo tomo*.   Fratelli Treves, Milano, 1927.   (First published in *The Bermondsey Book*, September 1926.)

CECCHI

EMILIO CECCHI was born at Florence in 1884. He began as a contributor to the *Voce*. He has been the literary critic of the *Tribuna* from 1910 to 1923. He now writes in the *Corriere della Sera*, and is a co-director of *Vita artistica*.

His principal works, in order of publication, are : *Rudyard Kipling* (1910), *Note d'arte a Valle Giulia* (1911), *La poesia di G. Pascoli* (1912), *Studi critici* (1912), *Storia della letteratura inglese*, 1° vol. (1915), *Pesci rossi* (1920), *La giornata delle belle donne* (1924), *Pittura italiana dell' Ottocento* (1926), *L'osteria del cattivo tempo* (1927), *I primitivi senesi* (1928), *Armando Spadini* (1928).

CAMBRIDGE

IT may have been because I arrived at Cambridge on the Thursday half-holiday, when the shops close at one, and the students put on blazers bearing the arms of their respective colleges and go out into the hockey fields. But I seemed to be arriving at one of those towns one goes to only in dreams. At a certain point, and several times during the day, I noticed that I was walking cautiously, on tip-toe, in order not to make a noise and not to awaken the little grey and deserted streets, the forsaken courts and lonely chapels—or myself.

It is a town of monasteries and a society of monasteries.

We, in Italy, are in the habit of thinking of our monasteries as being on the tops of our mountains ; we think of them as the head over the body, or as the diadem over the head. We feel the sense of solitude as mainly one of ascension, of reaching a pinnacle. A monastery on the top of one mountain calls to a yet higher monastery, one order calls to another, one saint to another. St. Francis calls to St. Dominic, St. Scolastica calls to St. Mary Magdalen. Between them, but infinitely below, lies an expanse of tilled fields, the sea with its fishermen at their nets, the cities with their men enclosed in houses.

Here solitude is spread out, it unfolds itself towards the horizon. It is a plain covered with cloisters ; and from one cloister you pass into another, and from that into yet another until you recognise, after having gone through a great many, all similar yet differing, a place whose confused and veiled identity would seem to be confirmed by some most distant memory, which is, however, only a few hours old. One realises, as if through the pure elements of geometry, a sense of solitude and seclusion from the world—like a man who stands amidst a colonnade and is unable to see anything around him, as far as the eye can reach, but shafts of columns, or like one who gazes fixedly at a chess-board. One passes from the quadrangle of one court to that of another by a magic stroke which, in an easy and surprising way, perpetually recombines the usual architectural and decorative themes : the ruddy tiles on the wall and the lead and glazing of the windows, the Jacobean Gothic arch and the serene arrises of the Italian Renascence, the rose of Lancaster and the Tudor portcullis, the soapy greenstone of the roofs and the malachite of the meadows.

And when one penetrates into these buildings through an endless succession of cells, libraries, refectories and chapels with oaken walls and ceilings and great porcelain-tiled fire-places, this symmetrical arrangement of space, silence and light becomes even more enchanted and, at times, gives one a feeling of quiet giddiness. On that day, a suggestion of thin mist gave the last touch to the picture. The hoar-frost crystals on the edges of the meadows added to the feeling of immobility and abstraction, as if even the grass tended to geometrise. Now and then, in the pale sky, the chime of a *carillon*, as distant as the bells in " Parsifal," would extend that atmosphere of meditation to the uttermost confines.

But more mysterious in quality and at the same time closer does this atmosphere become in the chapel of King's College. A green polar light from the nave windows brings to mind images of light in a submarine forest. In the dry and precise clarity of our climate, our columns and arches bear the weight of buildings with a logical economy of resources and with a sincere expres-

sion of human labour and resistance.   In this
denser atmosphere, things seem lighter, the effort
of supporting them not so great, and thus their
freedom of order and arrangement increases.
The column, which with us is an element of
strength and duty, becomes here one of elegance
and phantasy.   With us it is a serene slave of
stone.   In the chapel of King's College it is a
lively vegetation : it imitates the lanceolation of
leaves, it mounts and multiplies itself in veins and
stalks.   Our ceilings are static theorems, resolved
into naked lines of energy and beauty.   Here
the static theorem becomes a motive for the
creation of a heraldic vaulting or a flowery canopy.
But this free play of the imagination, this romantic
dreaming in stone does not occur except in a less
vivid reality, where some things have lost weight
merely because others, which establish their
relations of gravity, are more solid and heavy.
There is a greater freedom : in a poorer inter-
play of elements.
    Our architecture is the relation of stone and
air.   In the chapel of King's College, I am rather
led to feel the weaker, less dynamic relation of
plant and water.   And there is less scrupulous
care for style and beauty in this laxer relationship.
The statues on our noble buildings are almost
always noble ; but on these noble constructions
the statues are almost invariably grotesque.
Henry the Eighth, on the superb door of Trinity
College, stands unsteadily on his legs, with his
golden crown awry, as though he were a fairy

king. The rampant beasts on the mural coats-of-arms have smooth, tapering bodies like those of the chilly, hairless monsters that glide among the algæ. This luxuriant monotony, this leaden magnificence is indeed the North.

But how well must one be able to read and smoke a pipe in those little rooms neatly packed one behind each other in the labyrinths of the Colleges !

The path along which one goes to and fro from the world is lost. The noises of the world, as through the diver's helmet, only reach one through innumerable strata and densities. Recent books lie on the shelves, judged, as it were, in the ancient unmoving light of disconsolate time. The wonderment and the abstraction that transpire from the appearance of the place seem to affect the mind, and even the newest ideas must be received as materially fixed within an infinitely distant time.

I am not equal to the task of determining exactly the creative contribution of that culture to the world of to-day. I know, however, that more than half of the most vigorous names in contemporary English poetry, journalism and drama belong to men who had not the means to reside within those walls or else did not think it worth while to gain admission at the expense of the State. They are names of men who attended only the college of Life. For by lowering one's criterion of judgment one becomes limited, and a creative value, the only value that has any meaning in literature and philosophy, is then attributed to the exercise of activities which are noble without doubt, but of a social and external order. At this rate, one would end by allowing that even our universities, whose capacity to act as mere social organs may reasonably be doubted, contribute to the creative order of things.

For myself, I would always choose that other stern college ; the methods of discouragement rather than those of opportunity ; the difficulty of getting one book sooner than the library that offers ten thousand books. Intelligence being equal, I would choose the man who reads on a bus or in a garret, rather than he who reads in a Norman-Gothic cell or a Palladian library. The expositions of professors may be exceedingly subtle, but I believe that the commonplace criticism of life is more stringent. In short, I cannot but think that at Oxford and Cambridge one must end, in so far as art and humanity are concerned, by being drawn away from life and retiring into a superior æstheticism, although in a charming manner and realising all the exquisite lyrical capabilities of such a defect. Suggestive and venerable as is the antiquity of Cambridge, I know of antiquities even more suggestive and venerable in the Strand and in Fleet Street. In the pure and veiled scenery of Cambridge I can understand Gray. But to understand the great Coleridge, it is better to walk along the Embankment and through the black quarters of the press, where the atmosphere is charged with the smell of antimony and politics as the air of battlefields is with the odour of powder.

But apart from the teachings of experience, for which those exclusive conditions of work and practical collaboration present a different aspect, the function of the Oxford and Cambridge solitude is, from another point of view, quite genuine. There are men who, in the flower of their youth, suffered from the moral and material privations of our strangling modern life : and they will carry with them, transfused for ever into their physical nature, the memory of their difficulties and humiliations. There are men who spent these years of their life in a seminary near St. Peter's, passing each day over the flagstones of the Leonine city : they may end by becoming shepherds' priests or bolshevists and antichrists, but they will always bear within them the proud mark of holy Rome. There are men who, during these years, were near death and yet on the sea found their health again : they may grow old under the gas-light of an office, but the sea has left its salt in their soul and a reflex of its light under their brows. So it is with men who, in their youth, were at Oxford and Cambridge : they absorbed something indelible, as for me is the sense of poverty and for the shepherds' priest the glory of Rome. They absorbed something more lasting than an idea, for ideas are subject to compromise and change. Those men absorbed

an invulnerable sensation. They lived physically
in the native substance of their country during
their freshest years ; which is a very different
thing from knowing the same theoretically,
although indeed it may not exclude it. The
experience is quite a different matter ; it may
develop into an intellectual form, but there is
properly speaking nothing intellectual in it.
They became *English gentlemen* for life, as one may
become poor, Roman Catholic, or a son of the
sea. They were held, for a splendid hour, in a
kind of old-time visionary transfiguration, they
took part in a *pageant*, in a processional reality.
The arms carved on the doors of the colleges,
inlaid in the choir stalls, embroidered on the
hockey shirts, became a moral blazon for those
who had no heraldic one : they made them
members of one grand brotherhood of nobility.

Hence, when they came out into the world,
their ancient instinct for balance, their experienced
watchfulness, their confident, lordly and historical
patience, their calm dissembled pride ; that
virtus which, rather than an express and conscious
political wisdom, is a sense of resting one's feet
on a mighty foundation, and which of itself does
not in the least constitute virtue in a moral sense,
although it is certainly an immeasurable strength.
Hence that cautious dignity, which has known
how to give the most revolutionary tendencies
time and place to vent themselves and has been
able, while seeming to favour such tendencies,
to turn them away from their real aim ; that

cautious dignity, which has given a liberal and sometimes radical appearance to what is, in reality, the most conservative of politics, and has even bestowed an air of austerity, a detached and fatal authority on wrong-doing, pure and simple.

It is not difficult to understand why Labour should now attach so much importance to the conquest of these centres which mould the upper classes. This is one of the aims Labour is trying to achieve, before its ideas and forces are compromised, disarmed and finally immobilised, for heaven knows how many years, by one of their usual semblances of realisation.

From *Pesci Rossi*. Vallecchi, Firenze, 1920.
(First published in the *London Mercury*, January 1928.)

SERRA

RENATO SERRA was born at Cesena, in Romagna, in 1884. He studied first at Cesena and then at the University of Bologna, under Carducci. In 1907, he went to Florence, where he continued his literary studies at the then *Istituto Superiore*. He subsequently obtained the post of Italian master in the secondary school for girls at Cesena ; and in 1909, he was elected librarian of the Malatestian library in the same town.

He was called to arms in April 1915, and met his death in action on the Podgora, a hill overlooking the Isonzo, in July 1915. A bronze medal *al valore* was awarded to his memory.

His few works, none of them extensive, have been partly posthumous. In order of publication, they are : *Le lettere* (1914), *Esame di coscienza di un letterato* (1915), and *Scritti critici* (vol. 1, 1910 ; vols. 2 and 3, 1920).

SELF-EXAMINATION OF A MAN OF LETTERS

ONE would wish that between companions of an hour and of a passion something in common might remain for ever. But, it is impossible.

Everyone must go back to his own path, to his own past, and to his own sins.

We shall always come to the same conclusion :
War does not change anything. It doesn't
improve, it doesn't redeem and it doesn't wipe
out—by itself. It can work no miracles. It
cannot pay debts, it cannot wash away sins : in
this world of ours, which no longer believes in
a divine grace.

One's heart finds it hard to admit this. We
should like those who have toiled, suffered and
resisted for a cause, which must always be holy,
when one can undergo tribulation for its sake,
to come out of the trial as from a sacred font :
purer, every one of them. And they that
died, at least these we should like to see
enlarged, sanctified, without blemish and without
guilt.

But, no. Neither sacrifice nor death can add
anything to a life, to a work, to a heritage. The
work which a man has done remains what it is.
We should be lacking in that respect which is
due to him and his work if, in valuing it, we
brought to bear some extraneous criterion, some
vote of sympathy or rather of pity. That would
be an affront to one who has toiled seriously, to
one who died to accomplish his duty.

What is there, on this tired earth, that will have
changed, when it has drunk in the blood of so
great a slaughter : when the dead and wounded,
the tortured and the abandoned, shall sleep
together beneath the sod, while the grass above
will have become tender, bright and new, and

full of silent luxuriance in the Spring sun which is still unchanged ?

I am not prophesying ; I am merely looking at things as they are.

I am gazing at this earth, which has now the withered tints of Winter ; and, in fancy, I can almost see the silence exhaling in the form of a bluish vapour from the ruins of this world, lost in the frigid oblivion of empty spaces. I see the motionless clouds resting on the summits of the huddled and shrunken mountains, and under the vacant sky I can feel nothing but the weariness of the old white and worn roads lying in the midst of a sombre plain. I see no traces of mankind. The houses are small and scattered like débris ; a dull, opaque greenness has merged the furrows and paths into the monotony of the field ; there is neither sound nor voice, unless it be that of the lowering sky or of the rising fog, whose sluggish waves are as lifeless as cold ashes.

And yet life does persist, clinging to these ruins, inlaid in these furrows, hiding in these wrinkles, indestructible. One cannot see mankind, nor hear its ant-like swarming : it is a multitude of little beings lost in the squalor of the earth, who have been there so long that they have become part and parcel of the earth.

Centuries have followed upon centuries, and these herds of men have remained among the same mountains, amongst the same valleys : each in its own place, but with an endless shuffling and turmoil, which has however kept within the same boundaries. Peoples, nations and races have been encamped for almost two thousand years amidst the folds of this hardened crust. Fluxes and refluxes, sudden overflows and conquests, have from time to time submerged boundaries, swept whole districts, overturned, destroyed and changed : but how little, and for what a short time !

The traces of movements and transits have been worn away in the confused treading of our roads, and all around, in the fields, in the furrows, among the stones, Life has continued the same as ever ; it has always sprung up again from its hidden seeds, with that sameness of form, of language and of mysterious connections which, within a definite yet undefinable circuit, makes of so many distinct little beings an individual whole : a race, which renews throughout a hundred different generations the shapes of skulls which lie buried and unknown beneath the strata of the ageless earth, and perpetuates accents and unwritten laws.

What is a war, amidst these innumerable and tenacious creatures which continue to dig each one its own furrow, to tread each one its own path, to produce offspring upon the very sod which covers the dead ; which when interrupted, begin again, and when driven away, return ?

The War has brought in its wake devastation and confusion ; but millions of men are unaware of it. Individuals have fallen or fled ; but Life has remained, irreducible in its primitive and instinctive animality, for which the course of the sun and of the seasons is of more importance than all wars : passing hubbubs, dull blows, which mingle with all the remaining fatal travail and suffering of existence.

And after a hundred, after a thousand years, War beats once again on its return against the same dikes, and brings back to the same outlets the same human groups that had previously been driven or drawn from their abodes.

We are confronted to-day with the same old human tide which once flooded the plains of Russia and Germany, overflowed beyond the Rhine and into Flanders, and was routed at the mountain passes.

The fields of battle are the same, and the roads to them are the same.

It is true that this time a mighty, irresistible wave appears to have stirred up the most ancient strata of the humanity which is encamped in the regions of Europe : it is not a local adventure or disturbance, but a movement of entire peoples torn from their roots.

During the first days of the War, an undefinable impression was rife, that the time of the great floods, by which one race may take the place of another, had returned.   Europe had not seen such times for nearly two thousand years; and it was the Barbarians of old, the masses of the newer peoples, who began to move again from the places in which they had definitely settled when their tide had fallen back ; for, during the whole of this interval, partial movements and disturbances had not shifted them in a lasting manner.

Nor is it probable that they will be shifted even this time. Probably we shall not even have conquests of the kind which do not succeed in destroying the down-trodden vitality of a race, which gradually rises again like trampled grass and envelops, permeates and absorbs the foreign element, as occurred to the Germanic element which, having overflown into Western and Southern Europe, remained there when the invasions were over and was absorbed by our Latin countries.

One can already hear the opposite tides clashing and then flowing back from their line of impact, which is still unchanged. And in the end, everything will return more or less to its place. The War will have disposed of a situation which already existed ; it will not have created a new one.

But let us move ! Behind me, those that follow are all brothers, even if I do not see them or know them well.

I am satisfied with what we have in common, which is stronger than all that divides us. I am satisfied with the road which we shall have to tread together, which will bear us all equally ; and there will be but one step, one breath, one cadence, one destiny for us all. After the first miles of our marching, all differences will have fallen drop by drop like the perspiration from our downward looking faces, amidst the dragging of heavy feet and the growing heaviness of our breathing ; and then there will be only tired men who grow dejected, but gather new strength and proceed, without murmuring and without becoming enthusiastic : for it is so natural to do what one has to do.   There is no time for remembering the past or for thinking a great deal when we are moving shoulder to shoulder and there are so many things to be done, or rather, one thing only between us all.

Let us move together : one after the other, up the paths between the mountains, which smell of broom and mint.   We defile upwards like ants upon a wall, and finally we cautiously peep over the mountain ridge in the silence of the morning. Or let us move together in the evening along great wide roads, soft with dust, which muffle and multiply the tramping of feet in the darkness, while above there gleams the faint, silvery-green thread of the new moon, right up in between the small, white, virgin stars of April ; when if one halts, one can feel on one's neck the warm breath of the column closing up behind.   Or, at night, let us sleep together a sleep that is buried in the depths of the black, frozen sky ; and later, feel in our sleep the mournful weeping of the morning dew, as subtle as the flaw in a crystal ; and then : up, for the day is already breaking. So : marching and halting together, resting and rising together, toiling and remaining silent together ; files and files of men which follow the same track, tread the same soil, a dear, hard, solid and eternal soil, firm under our feet and good for our bodies.   And then there are all the other things of which one does not speak, because one must be there to understand them, and then one feels them, and in a manner which makes words useless.

From *Esame di coscienza di un letterato*.
(Fratelli Treves, Milano, 1916.)

JAHIER

PIERO JAHIER was born at Genoa in 1884. By profession he is an employee of the Italian state railways. He became known through his contributions to the *Voce*, and published his first important work, *Risultanze in merito alla vita e al carattere di Gino Bianchi*, in 1912. During the War, Jahier served as an officer in the Alpine Corps, and edited the *Astico*, a periodical of the trenches. He is the author of a fine collection of soldiers' songs, *Canti di soldati*, published in 1918. After the War, he founded *Il nuovo contadino*, a review for the Italian agricultural labourer. But his two principal works are *Ragazzo* (1919) and *Con me e cogli Alpini* (1919), the first an autobiographical reminiscence of his early youth, and the second a series of War impressions derived from his experiences in the Alpine Corps.

CRITICISM

THEY *criticise* me because I am so much with the men.
Even after hours.
But these are men who improve their officers.
It is in order to improve myself that I remain with them.
I endeavour to get into this manly resignation, into this cheerful courage of theirs.

Besides, one's real duties begin after hours, beyond discipline.

This is a work of love : to this alone will credit be given.

So—when drill is over—I go and hear what they are thinking about in the men's quarters.

I joke about their short laundry list.

I take an interest in the worn shoe, in the letter that ought to have arrived.

I squeeze out the black pimple.

I also assist at the inoculation : that they may offer their chests boldly, and, steadying their gaze in mine, not tremble, no, not one of them, when the needle pierces ; that they may calmly salute when their first blood is drawn.

They *criticise* me because I taste each mess tin, and not only once.

They say it is ostentation. The victualling is after all always the same.

But no rations are the same, even though the victualling may be.

They differ as to salt, they differ in degree of cooking : and he can gauge this difference, the soldier who eats nothing but his ration, and has the fresh appetite of the whole body, not of the stomach only, like the spoilt civilian.

They *criticise* me because I share too much with the common soldier.

Nay more, I would share my ration, I would share my paillasse with him.

It would be right and fitting.

In war, he who has less needs is superior.

In this the army officer is not superior.

In this the officer is inferior.

If there is anyone who needs to inure himself to privation, it is not the common soldier : it is just the officer, who comes from his three meals at home, from his tidy bed.

These men have been inuring themselves to privation for thirty years.

If anything they would need to be cared for, to be fostered by their country.

" But what about authority ? . . . But what about prestige ? "

I admit that food is a matter of great intimacy.

But, nevertheless, you eat with your father or with your captain.

In fact, a man who eats the same as another has only the prestige of his soul left as a distinction.

By eating together with the men you would feel the need of this prestige.

And what you could save would mean field-glasses or an aneroid—besides health.

This is real superiority : to earn one's leadership among them.

Again they criticise, saying : " To the ignorant, authority is stars and rank. It works simply and convincingly : stars and—cells."

Certainly : that is the discipline of peace, and it has been an aid to marching along elbow to elbow on parade in the open square.

But now it is a case of going to die, scattered and far apart, on the Alps.

That was a comfortable discipline : one of imposition—good enough if you are content to see caps moving round together.

But *I* see, beneath these caps, the noble faces of the Italian people. The intelligent faces of this tried people arrest my attention, the faces which think, like Gioietta, while you are imposing your will :

" Ah ! you strike me because you are big, don't you ? . . . but you hurt me : I am small, you know. . . . You make me obey because you have stars and a code."

Look to yourself, because the true discipline of danger is now born and growing ; it was born at the front, where one does not salute this bespangled superior, but where one treads on his feet and laughs at him.

Now we are going towards death. It is a road without lies.

Still they criticise, and someone turns at my salute, ready to jump to attention.

" You frightened me—why it's only a common soldier ! And you salute him better than you would the general ! "

No—but I salute his duty to obey, which is equal to my duty to command.

These duties are equal, therefore the salute is equal.

Besides, it is a common soldier I know well.

I do not know his Excellency, the General, well.

They are always criticising me because I keep company with my inferiors.

But I am not keeping company with my inferiors : I associate with my equals.

You think you are better informed because you have been through the schools, and that the soldiering populace is inferior to you.

You think that wisdom depends upon the alphabet—and nobility upon the tailor.

But *I* do not believe all these things.

You, what has your life been hitherto ?

You were born, you have filled skin, emptied skin and rubbed skin.

Then your uncle, Head of Division, gave you a job.

And since then you have filled more skin, emptied more skin and rubbed skin better.

And if you talk to me you cannot find anything else to talk about but this filling, emptying and rubbing of skin which for you has been life.

So I would sooner have the company of my peasant trumpeter.

Who has a soul so rich that it overflows into poetry, when he relates to me the struggle against want which has been his life.

The travels and battles of an Italian peasant against want.

And he brings before me the nights on board the steamer, when he used to sleep on the boiler

and the dishes made music to keep him company ;
and he lets me see the life-boat during a ship-
wreck : how, at the heaving of the waves, it rose
like a little bird.

I accompany him to where he worked among
the negroes, who are fond of the gentle Italians
because they let them pass on the pavement and
do not make them walk, like horses, in the middle
of the road.   I go back with him to the time when
he accepted even the most toilsome tasks : ten
hours under water, going down to look for the
sand bank, so that the steamer might be able to
pass ; and he used to carry the mouth of the
sand-pump with him to the bank and then clang
three times to let them know that the mouth had
to suck.

And he has put aside in three years a clear
five thousand five hundred *lire*, honestly earned.

But never did he lose either his zest for work
or his appetite.

Not even on the festivals, when his countrymen
used to spend freely.   He would find an excuse
to remain all alone—in that foreign place.

And in his native place, he had prepared a little
house—a new one—so that he might take a wife
and that no one might laugh when he had,
" because I have nowhere to take her."

Instead of which the War came ; and the
house, which had only just been roofed, was
closed and his wife had gone back to her father.

But when she goes to town for her allowance,
she calls at the new house among the brambles

and smuggles away in the drawer five *lire* or so for her husband.

Because, afterwards, she does not want him to cross the Ocean again : if he survives this wicked War.

She took him during his winter leave to the closed house, and opened the drawer to give him a surprise.

He smiles like an angel and tears come into his eyes when he tells me about his good wife.

He has always been true to her ; he has never touched another woman.

But if he survives, he will go back to America all the same to complete his fortune : a proper man like himself must have some land round his house.

And he has some grape-shot in his body, you know.

Oh yes ! I do indeed associate with this inferior of mine.

When I have been in his company, I feel solaced.

And I pray for him that he may return to his wife—and to his country, that he may bring up his children for himself—and for his country.

But you, who are superior, go if you will to your own fate.

And also keep away from him.

If he obeys you it is because you keep away from him.

His respect is based on the belief that rank is justice, that it is merit, that it is reward.

Perhaps he believes you have earned your rank.
Woe if he should lose this belief !

Woe if he really knew what you are !

In order to serve your country you must keep far away from him : as far as when he was under water looking for that sand bank, and you were in the 'Corso' powdering your fancy shoes with dust.

They laugh because 'Giaiè' is always standing to attention.

They laugh because 'Giaiè' is always reading 'King's Regulations' : 'Giaiè,' whose only fault lies in taking everything seriously.

But you remember to *do good desperately.* If it were done with pleasure, who would not do it ?

It is good precisely because it *is* done desperately ; because it is done at all costs, in disregard of whatever may be thought of it.

And, for the rest, calmly open your furrow and let fall your seed.

Both wind and sun are of God.

From *Con me e con gli alpini.* ('La Voce,' Soc. An. Ed., Roma, 1920.)

NEGRI

ADA NEGRI was born in 1870 at Lodi, in Lombardy. She has been a schoolmistress, first in the country schools of Motta Visconti and then at Milan. Some early poems of hers were published when she was only seventeen. She formerly contributed to the *Secolo*, and now contributes regularly to the *Corriere della Sera*. Her works are mainly poetical ; in fact it was only during the War that she began to write in prose.

Her publications are, in chronological order, the following collections of poems : *Fatalità* (1892), *Tempeste* (1894), *Maternità* (1906), *Dal profondo* (1910), *Esilio* (1914), *Il libro di Mara* (1919), and the following volumes of lyrical prose, partly essayistic and partly autobiographical : *Le solitarie* (1917), *Orazioni* (1918), *Stella mattutina* (1921), *Finestre alte* (1923), *Le strade* (1926), and *Sorelle* (1928).

THE STORY OF LADY AUGUSTA

LEFT a widower with an only daughter of fifteen, who was then being educated in a convent, Count Giorgione Dauli, moved by a late love-caprice—he being already nearly fifty—had married a young teacher of that same convent.

A novice without any vocation, who had been

forced into the cloister by the pretentious poverty
of her family, the young teacher thought herself
very fortunate in being able to leave the nunnery
for a country house.

Physically, she was a superb creature, with
black hair and the profile of a Roman empress,
which concealed, however, the brain of a bird.

After their marriage, the Count took his wife
to his ancestral palace at Lodi. And there they
kept up with great pomp and expenditure a
fantastic succession of balls and receptions, a
perpetual transition from splendour to splendour.

This was at the time of the festivities for the
coronation of Bonaparte, the First Consul, who
had become Emperor, when the aristocracy of
Lombardy seemed to have been smitten with a
mania for dancing, luxury and pleasure.

The Countess Francesca was feeling the first
symptoms of approaching maternity ; but, appar-
ently subservient to the wishes of her husband,
she did not on this account renounce a single
ball.

Sometimes, while descending in great magnificence of dress the wide marble steps of the
palace to the *berlina* (1) waiting at the door, she
would be assailed by that feeling of sickness and
nausea natural to her condition, and would try
by bending forward to spare her splendid white
satin bodice, made in the latest fashion and
powdered with diamonds.

But the Count her husband, inexorable,

1. A large four-wheeled carriage. Cp. the French : *berline*.

holding her up by her arm and speaking from
above his aldermanic corporation, would cry :
" Upright ! . . . Upright ! . . . By St. George !
Upright, Countess ! . . . Count Dauli has money
for other dresses ; but the little Count must be
born well made ! . . . Keep your head up, Lady
Francesca ! "

And Lady Francesca, obeying, would vomit
on to the white satin bodice powdered with
diamonds.

In due time a son was born who, however, died
immediately, to the great despair of both his
parents.   Then, some years afterwards, Augusta
was born.

Her mother never loved her.   For some way-
ward reason she loved her dead son, and him
only.   A smouldering rancour, also inexplicable,
alienated her from her husband : almost as if
he had been the cause of the loss of their first-
born.   Augusta grew up amidst the petty gossip
of the servants' hall, and spent her time between
the wardrobe, the kitchen and the stables.

At seven years of age she was put into a
college ; while Lady Sandra, the daughter of the
Count by his first wife, was given in marriage to
a gentleman living in the neighbourhood of
Cremona.

Then the Count and Countess, their fortune
greatly diminished by the mad dissipation of
nearly twenty years, retired to a villa surrounded
by farms, which yet remained to them.

They still gave in all good faith the name of

love to the most passionate conjugal hatred that ever held together a man and a woman.

At intervals, angry disputes would break out between the two—especially over money matters. After each one of these, Count Giorgione, deafened by the hysterical abuse of his wife, would decamp, desperately dragging his round body on its short legs through corridors and salons, and knotting round his head, as though in defence, a large silk handkerchief with red and yellow squares ; while the Countess Francesca would rush out all dishevelled into the garden, and seizing a pair of garden scissors would flourish them over flowers and branches, crying :

" I will cut ! . . . I will cut ! . . . I will cut the knot ! . . ."

Nor did these scenes cease when Lady Augusta, having completed her eighteenth year, returned home from college.

To describe the Lady Augusta as beautiful would not be saying much. Many women are beautiful—but the Lady Augusta was beauty itself.

She had inherited the plasticity of her mother, together with her heavy blue-black hair, besides the pearly skin and the long oval face of the Daulis ; yet the secret of her charm did not lie in all this ; nor in her wonderfully large eyes or in her exquisitely small mouth.

Perhaps she wore an enchanted ring, like some of the princesses in fairy tales. She spoke but seldom : and rarely smiled. She was, moreover,

very ignorant. While at the ' Istituto Garnier'
in Milan, the most aristocratic and fashionable
College of the time, she had—to tell the truth—
only learnt how to dance and sweep the most
graceful curtsies, and how to move and hold her
head like a goddess. So much so, that from
time to time the Count her father, raising his
short, stumpy arms to heaven, would exclaim :
" Ah, Madame Garnier, the money I have
wasted upon you ! " . . . Ignorant, yes. But
whoever saw her once, never forgot her.

In haste they betrothed her to the Baron Otto
von Löwenthal, a wealthy Austrian officer in
garrison at Cremona. No one asked her if she
really loved him. She allowed them to put the
betrothal ring on her finger, to congratulate her,
to lavish gifts upon her, without saying anything
or ever losing for a moment that attitude of an
impassive idol which so much added to her
beauty. But he, yes, he was madly in love with
her. And when the sudden death of his father
recalled him to Vienna to set in order the complica-
tions of an almost princely inheritance, he felt
heart-broken at having to say Good-bye to his
betrothed ; but scrupulously correct as he was,
he did not allow any of his suffering to appear.

He was to return in six or seven months' time.
He wrote every day ; and every night he dreamt
of his beloved and longed for her.

In the meantime, Lady Augusta, in order to
drive away her sadness, and according to the
custom of the time, was sent by her parents on a

visit of some weeks to the house of a friend :
the Marquis Savelli, of Pontevico.   A married
nobleman, and the father of a bunch of sturdy
children, he was still young in years, of a comely
appearance and gallant in manners.   His name
was Arnoldo : and he was a formidable hunter
and swordsman.   Just at that time his house was
gay with many guests.

When by chance he was seen by the side of the
Lady Augusta, the same idea struck everyone
present : that they seemed to be blood relations.
They appeared to be more closely related than
even brother and sister.   Is this possible ? . . .
If there is a tie of consanguinity closer and more
mysteriously tyrannical, then between those
two it certainly existed.

When near to each other, even in the midst
of a crowd of other people, an invisible wall, a
barrier of air, seemed to separate them from
everyone else.

The harmony of her form, in its fullness of line
and colour, the rhythm of her movements, the
significance of her few words and of her long
silences, suited him, penetrated sympathetically
into his inmost being and rested there, obeying
a natural law that was stronger than either reason
or will.

When they went hunting, he on his black
courser and she on her white, both of them daring
to the degree of foolhardiness, they made those
who saw them think of the fables of the centaurs :
such an appearance had they of splendid animal-

ity, and so firm was their seat in the saddles of their mounts. They formed that perfect and yet undefinable couple, which from time to time, perhaps once in a century, Nature is pleased to create—and man to destroy.

The Marquis Savelli had the misfortune to possess a little blonde wife, who was also a great gossip ; indeed through her excessive, brainless chatter she had enlarged the veins of her neck. And on the other hand, the Lady Augusta was betrothed to the Baron of Löwenthal. When, however, their eyes met, neither of the two was able to remember these things.

One night, in Villa Savelli, the shrieks and cries of a woman were heard ; these were immediately suffocated, and there followed a slamming of doors and the sound of dragging footsteps in the corridors. Then, a heavy silence and the suspension of all life until dawn.

At break of day, a closed carriage, laden also with the baggage of the Lady Augusta, took the young Countess, accompanied by her maid, back to her parents. The latter did not demand a full explanation of the sudden return of their daughter; but were content with some excuse invented on the spur of the moment, which, however, was plainly miles from the truth. They probably had not the courage to go to the bottom of the matter, to insist on the truth, when confronted by that impassive and marmoreal face.

Remorse, in its most obscure and rudimentary form, gnawed perhaps for a moment at their conscience : and this they found it easiest to stifle with silence. Thus they continued their twilight existence, broken only by the usual noisy quarrels, after which the old Count would grumblingly wrap up his bald head in the silk handkerchief chequered with red and yellow squares, which the servants now called "the handkerchief of the *baruffe*" (squabbles) ; while the Countess Francesca, her still black hair all rumpled and falling over her shoulders, would run hither and thither among the paths of the garden, brandishing her garden scissors and crying : " I will cut ! . . . I will cut ! . . . I will cut the knot ! " . . .

Her daughter, also, would often go down into the garden ; but alone, and only when she was certain that no one was following her. Penetrating into the closest thickets of the trees and bushes, she would choose and gather with great care certain herbs, wherewith, in her own room, she afterwards compounded strange mixtures, which she would swallow surreptitiously at certain fixed hours, murmuring the while strange spells and making the sign of the cross.

She herself, as time went on, acquired something of the colour of those green herbs. Her gaze became more and more lost in vacancy ; but she never complained, and to whomsoever asked of her how she did, she would reply, suddenly widening her mouth into a brilliant smile such as might have been produced by the action of an internal spring : " I ? . . . Very well indeed."

But the splendour of her teeth disappeared at once behind lips immediately resealed.

Nothing more was heard of the Savellis, and no one in the house ever spoke of them.

At regular intervals there arrived passionate letters from Baron von Löwenthal at Vienna : sometimes two or three together ; and at rarer intervals, there departed for Vienna letters from the Lady Augusta, short, almost infantile, and sprinkled with grammatical errors, like early school compositions.

Thus passed several months.

But Lady Augusta's maid, while helping her to dress in the morning and to undress at night, began to remark with quiet respect, which scarcely concealed an anxious pity :

" *Contessina*, we must have the belts of your dresses enlarged. Do you know, we are getting fat ! "

To which the Lady Augusta, without looking at her, invariably replied : " Don't be foolish, Marianì ! . . . You must be dreaming ! . . ."

But the faithful Marianì was not foolish, and sighing she muttered to herself :

" If only I were ! . . . Or if only my young lady had just a little more confidence in this poor fool who saw her born, so many things could perhaps be remedied in time."

But when the eldest daughter of Count Giorgione gave a grand ball at Cremona on the last Saturday in Carnival, to attend which the Lady Augusta came up from the country with Marianì, her faithful attendant tried in vain, two hours before the dance began, to fasten the waist of her young mistress's gown.

The dress was a dream : it was made of the lightest pink gauze, with innumerable flounces trimmed with maidenhair.

" *Contessina*, it is impossible. And only a few months ago it fitted you perfectly, do you remember ? . . . At that reception in the house of the Savellis, at Pontevico. Now it is quite impossible to fasten it."

" Yes, it can . . . it *must* be fastened. Squeeze, squeeze, Mariani ! . . ."

" Do you want to die, my Lady ? . . . Do you really wish me to kill you ? . . . I, who saw you born, and held you in my arms when you were a baby. And when you had that dreadful fever, night and day you would have none but me. Be good ; have confidence in your poor old servant. Are you ill ? . . . Do you not see ? . . . If I squeeze any more I shall break your ribs. . . ."

" Squeeze, squeeze, Mariani ! . . ."

Squeezing and pulling, pulling and squeezing, the hooks at last met, and the dress was fastened ; and Mariani drew back, regarding her own work with terror, as one regards an instrument of torture.

But the young Countess, although her face was whiter than her white satin shoes, laughed triumphantly, only with a laugh which sounded like the rasping of a blade on glass.

" Have we succeeded or no ? . . . Oh you simpleton of a Marianì ! " . . .

And she made her fasten a bunch of jessamine in her belt, and a crown of the same flowers on her hair, which was so thick and lustrous as to seem almost of a solid substance ; pretending not to notice that the hands of her old maid trembled. Then she went down to the ball-room and danced.

She danced with all comers ; passing without interruption from one cavalier to another, from one dance to another, like some marvellous mechanical doll, which an invisible hand wound up at the end of every round. Everybody saw her smiling : a fixed brilliant smile, that seemed painted on her face ; but few heard her speak.

Now and then, she put her hand to her waist, perhaps to replace the bunch of jessamine disarranged by the exertion of the dance. She grew paler and paler ; even her lips became white.

" Lady Augusta, will you have a lemonade ? "

" No, let us dance."

" Lady Augusta, are you tired ? . . . Shall we rest a little : there, in the red drawing-room? "

" No, let us dance."

Ever paler ; but with two sinister blotches of red under her eyes : until, towards three o'clock in the morning, while turning to the music of a waltz in the arms of the Duke Visconti Arese, she fell heavily to the ground, and was carried away. It was impossible to unfasten her dress. But, extending her on a bed in one of the most remote rooms of the palace, where not even the echoes of the dance could be heard, they cut the dress on her body ; and then her poor, tortured, swollen figure immediately sprang out, revealing itself as nakedly as a confession.

She did not speak. Only, from her throat there came a continual, suppressed groan, always the same—the wail of a dying animal :

" O-oh ! . . . O-oh ! . . . O-oh ! "

It was clear that even in the state of unconscious agony into which she had fallen, she would have liked to suffocate even that cry ; but she could not.

The family physician, who had been secretly sent for and introduced into the palace like a thief, through a servants' door, was unable to say or do anything. She lay dying because she had wished to die : silently suffocating in her own blood, in the consequences of her own passion.

Nothing more issued from her lips, except that one syllable which tore the hearts of her relations and of poor Marianì bending over her :

" O-oh ! . . . O-oh ! . . . O-oh ! " . . .

But towards the evening of that same day even those " O-ohs " froze on her lips, and she remained motionless.

Thus passed out of life the Lady Augusta.

Her father and mother wept for her with great clamour. But when he knew all, the Baron von Löwenthal slew the image of her within his heart, just as though she were not dead already.

Then they forgot her.

But she who quickly followed, because she could not live without her, was the old Marianì.

From *Stella mattutina*. (A. Mondadori, Milano, 1921.) (By kind permission of the author.)

BONTEMPELLI

MASSIMO BONTEMPELLI was born at Como in
1884. He began his career as a teacher of
Italian Language and Literature in secondary
schools. In 1910 he took up journalism and
became in succession sub-editor of the Florentine
Cronache letterarie, editor of the *Marzumsca*, and
contributor to the *Secolo* and to the *Mondo*. In
1922 he abandoned journalism in order to devote
himself entirely to independent work, some of
which now appears in the *Gazzetta del Popolo*.

His works include many different *genres*, but
it is essentially upon his short stories that his
reputation has been founded. His principal
publications are the following collections of
poems, essays and short stories : *Egloghe* (1904),
Odi siciliane (1906), *Socrate moderno* (1908),
Amori (1910), *Odi* (1910), *Sette savi* (1912),
S. Bernardino da Siena (1914), *Dallo Stelvio al
mare* (1915), *Meditazione intorno alla guerra
d'Italia e d'Europa* (1917), *Maria Melato* (1919),
Il puro sangue ; *L'Ubriaco* (1919), *La vita intensa*
(1920), *La vita operosa* (1920), *Viaggi e scoperte*
(1922), *La scacchiera davanti allo specchio* (1922),
Eva ultima (1923), *La donna del Nadir* (1924),
La donna dei miei sogni (1925), *La donna nel sole
ed altri idilli* (1928), *Il Neosofista e altri scritti*
(1928), *Il figlio di due madri* (1929), and the
following plays : *La guardia alla luna* (1916),
Siepe a nordovest (1919), *Nostra Dea* (1925),
Minnie la candida (1927).

STRAW AND HAY

I WAS living in the country, and every day, towards dusk, I used to take a walk along certain lanes which led out on to the main road.

One evening, coming out on to the main road together with my lane, I saw at a certain distance, enveloped in the first shades of twilight, what appeared to be an enormous square-shaped animal resting on the road near the edge of the grass. I could not very well distinguish its outlines, which were, however, thick and heavy. It lay quite still ; but I very soon noticed that underneath it, along the ground, something was moving, and it was not the animal itself : it was another animal, narrower and longer, a reptile of large proportions which, lying under the larger animal, partially protruded itself and now and then agitated the protruding part to and fro in the dust. I therefore supposed that the reptile was sucking at the breast of the square-shaped monster. This would have accounted for the latter's stillness. But upon drawing closer full of curiosity, I at once perceived that I had been guilty of a zoological error : the larger animal was only a motor-car suffering from a breakdown, while the reptile which was squirming under its breast was the driver, all enveloped in an over-all, who, lying on his back and looking upwards, was not sucking, but probing with his hands the mysterious mechanism.

While I was digesting my disillusion, another personage appeared, emerging like a dryad from behind a tree. I saw at once that it was a man. I understood that he was the owner of the motor-car and, furthermore, I recognised in him a friend of mine : Adalgiso. With a brief and rapid series of 'Ohs' and 'Ahs' and other ritual formulæ, we went through the usual appropriate ceremony for two persons who meet at an un-expected time or place. Then Adalgiso confided to me :

"As soon as it can go, I shall get in again."

"I had surmised that much," I replied.

"And I shall go back to town."

"This also I had suspected."

"And you shall come with me."

Adalgiso is an imperious friend, I a docile one. Nevertheless, for the sake of my dignity, I asked : "Why ? "

Adalgiso explained : "Because I say so."

I should probably have not raised any objec-tions. But he deigned to explain the matter even further :

"You must come with me, because it is absolutely necessary for me to reach town this evening. To-day I have already had two or three breakdowns. Now you are a good mascot. Come along and be my mascot for these last twenty miles. If you don't come, who knows what may yet happen to me ! "

"And if I do come ? "

"Then everything will go smoothly.   We shall get home towards dark.   I shall go about my business and you about yours.   I am sorry I cannot put you up at home, but I will tell you the names of the principal hotels.   To-morrow morning, at six o'clock, you can return by train."

"Look," I interrupted, "he has finished." For the reptile was crawling out ; it raised itself upon its hands and feet, thus becoming, for a fleeting instant, a quadruped ; then with a vigorous jerk of the upper part of its body it became a biped, and the visor of its cap looked towards the heavens, the dwelling-place of God : it was a man.

"What was the matter ? " asked Adalgiso.

"I really couldn't say," grumbled the driver.

"Will you be much longer repairing it ? " insisted Adalgiso.

The driver merely shrugged his shoulders. Whereupon I said resolutely to Adalgiso : "We can get in.   It is ready."

"How ? "

"Let's get in, I say."

We got in ; the driver took his seat, pushed and pressed, and behold : the car shook and started.

"I have always said," remarked Adalgiso with admiration, "that you were an extraordinary man."

But my self-assurance was simply the result of former observation.

I had observed that whenever a born engineer

affirms : " It's the carburettor. It's a mere
trifle," or " It's a dirty plug. In ten minutes
we shall have everything in order," and similar
precise, localising, technical phrases of a re-
assuring nature, there invariably follow hours of
vain researches and attempts around the inanim-
ate machine. When, on the other hand, the
engineer confines himself to a sceptical and
generic grumbling, all one has to do is to turn the
starting handle or press a button, and the breakdown is at an end.

Nevertheless, I let Adalgiso believe in my
magical virtues as a mascot.

And I set myself to invigilate the journey
with the closest attention, in order to respond
worthily to Adalgiso's faith in me and in the
supernatural.

The car was running as placidly as a comet.
After a short silence, Adalgiso spoke :

" I have lived for thirty-seven years without
ever noticing this extremely simple fact : that
when the thirteenth of the month falls on a
Friday, the seventeenth falls on a Tuesday."

I reckoned this up in my mind, and then said :
" That's true."

" And you had never thought of it ! No one
has ever thought of it. I have been the first."

" Bravo ! "

I again concentrated upon the journey, while
the motor-car continued to fly over the smooth
road, which now ran alongside a little river and
between two rows of pale poplars. In the sky,

which was still bright, a slice of a moon was being served.   At the sound of our flight, the shadows issued from the thickets bordering the fields and ran along the road, and hung on closely to the moving car.

"Go a little slower," said Adalgiso to the driver.

Then he settled down more comfortably into his corner and remained silent ; only now and then did he murmur a word or so, which before I could succeed in catching it would fly away and hide itself among the new shadows which were fast closing in on either side of us.

At a certain point the car, slowing down a little, moved over to the right side of the road. I, who was sitting on the left, half lowered the window on my side and leaned out to look. I saw that advancing towards us was a cart with an immense square-shaped load.   Now Adalgiso from his seat had also caught sight of it, and he said to me : " Note carefully what it is : straw or hay ? "—His voice was shaking.

I had not yet answered, when the cart passed us by and Adalgiso suddenly cried in great glee : " It's hay ! It's hay ! That brings luck."

I shuddered.   Because Adalgiso had made a mistake : I had seen most distinctly that the cart was laden with straw, which is unlucky. But I did not wish to undeceive him.   And now there passed another cart.

"More hay ! " shouted Adalgiso.

Whereas it was again straw : and it had brushed against the car. I, in the darkness within, felt red with vexation and pale with fright ; and at the same time the illusion in which Adalgiso was lulling himself made me feel sorry for him.

Yet another cartload of straw did he salute as hay. I trembled lest his confidence should increase the baneful influence of the straw. But I had not the heart to destroy his splendid enthusiasm.

A dramatic conflict was being waged within me, and I could not see any solution to it.

This conflict did not even express itself in voice or movement : as the storm in my intimate consciousness became more violent and my sense of responsibility more painful, I grew stiller and stiller and pressed harder and harder against the cushions. I felt that we were approaching a catastrophe, and I writhed in my impotence to avoid it and in the conviction that I was abetting it by my dastardly silence.

And now, in the distant shadows, there appeared the shape of another cart with an extremely high load.

" Let us be sure that this is not straw," said Adalgiso, " it might spoil the effect of the other three cartloads."

I strained forward my sight, my attention, my whole being : and I saw, oh I saw unmistakably —even from a distance—that this time it really was hay.

It was drawing nearer. In a flash, I realised
that in order to destroy the preceding spell, that
thrice repeated spell, which had been strengthened
by the facile faith of Adalgiso, it was not enough
to allow the hay to pass us by. Some more
potent ritual was required. It was required
that I should succeed in seizing some of that
hay to carry along with us in the rushing motor-
car. I resolved to snatch it as we passed and to
throw it into the arms of Adalgiso. This alone
would suffice to counteract all the previous spells.

The cart was now very near and towering
above us. My heart was beating wildly.

Here it was. But the window had only been
lowered half way. This was not enough ; so
while I was leaning forward and stretching out
my right hand in readiness for the theft, I
pressed down vigorously with my left the edge of
the bevelled glass window. I pressed so forcibly
with my left hand that the thick glass broke in
pieces. At the same instant I seized and pulled
away with my right hand a tuft of hay.

The car passed on and the cart disappeared
at once behind us. With a joyful cry I turned
and threw the hay onto Adalgiso.

" What the devil have you done ? " he asked.

" Why," I replied, " I have cut my hand.
Hurrah ! " And with my handkerchief I glee-
fully began to mop the blood which was oozing
out of my palm.

" Yes," said Adalgiso, " but I was referring to
the glass."

The car was continuing its flight over the empty road and was already making eyes at the first houses of the town. Breathlessly I vented myself and explained everything to Adalgiso.

" It was straw, it was all straw, at first ; straw in the first, second and third carts. I did not dare to tell you : you were so pleased ! I suffered atrociously. Now my task is accomplished. Express your gratitude !

" And now I see it all quite plainly. The intervention of that handful of hay has reduced to a minimum, to the breaking of a wretched piece of glass, all the harm of the preceding evil omen. But for that hay, we would probably have met with a catastrophe. We have arrived. Keep that hay, Adalgiso, and take it with you on all your motoring tours."

" ' Wretched ' glass ? " he was muttering. " Not so ' wretched,' I think ! "

He accompanied me to an hotel and recommended me to the porter. Affectionately laying a little of the hay in his pocket-book, he wished me good-bye, saying :

" You are even lucky in having injured your left hand. If it should remain disabled, you still have your right hand for writing your pretty little stories."

From *La donna dei miei sogni*. (A. Mondadori, Milano, 1925.) (By kind permission of the author.)

BACCHELLI

RICCARDO BACCHELLI was born at Bologna in 1891. He began as a contributor to the *Patria* of Bologna and to the *Voce* of Florence.

More recently he has contributed to the *Ronda* of Rome, to the *Fiera Letteraria* and to the *Italia Letteraria*.

He has also written novels, short stories, plays and poems.

His principal works, in chronological order, are the following novels and collections of short stories : *Il filo meraviglioso di Lodovico Clò* (1910), *Memorie del tempo presente* (1919–21), *Lo sa il tonno* (1923), *Il Diavolo al Pontelungo* (1927), *La ruota del tempo* (1928), *Bella Italia* (1928), *La città degli amanti* (1929), *Acque dolci e Peccati* (1930) ; the following plays : *Spartaco e gli schiavi* (1920), *Presso i termini del destino* (1922), *Amleto* (1923), *La notte di un nevrastenico* (1925), *La smorfia* (1926), *La famiglia di Figaro* (1926), *Bellamonte* (1928) ; a collection of poems : *Poemi lirici* (1914), and a critical selection, with introduction and notes, of Ippolito Nievo's best work : *Le più belle pagine di Ippolito Nievo* (1929).

THE TWO VIOLINS

THE art of the novelist is philosophical, because it reveals in minute cases the laws which govern great events. Thus this short story will end philosophically, with a question.

Along the Emilian Way (1), from the Po to the *Ponte d'Augusto* at Rimini, one understands what the love of Italian opera really is.

It was not without good reason that Verdi was born at Busseto and the father of Rossini came from Lugo in Romagna. This love exhales from the taverns and from beneath the porticoes in songs and serenades, it waxes enthusiastic in the galleries of the theatres, it wastes itself in envious rivalry between town and town, and rages within the musical factions.

To-day, amidst the universal levelling down of things, the passion for Italian opera is also on the decline, but there are still fine remnants of it.

Only this could explain how the last of the second violins, there being no third violins in the orchestra, in the municipal and once ducal theatre of an Emilian town, a fellow nicknamed Thou Sufferest, could possibly make a living out of his art, of which he was supremely ignorant. Only this passion could account for the creation of a party in his favour on the memorable occasion of his quarrel with the impresario Bagatti.

In truth Thou Sufferest, in accordance with his ungrammatical nickname (2), would have bent his shoulders beneath the harshness and abuse

1. The old *Via Æmilia*, a continuation of the *Via Flaminia*. It runs right through the modern Emilia, from Piacenza, on the Po, to Rimini on the Adriatic coast.

2. In the Italian original: *Soffrisci*. This is a whimsical perversion of *soffri*, second person singular of the present indicative of *soffrire*, to suffer.

of that overbearing man.   But others litigated
for him, and among the foremost his friend and
orchestral colleague Corrado Barbatinca, the last
but one of the second violins, called, when he
was not within hearing, Smelly Head.   For fifty
years he had been at loggerheads with the whole
town on account of this nickname, with the
result that it had stuck fast to him.   From father
to son the Barbatincas had sold pilchards and
anchovies in a small shop under the portico of
the market.   The nickname, derived from the
well-known property of fish, had been transmitted
along with the barrels of pickles and the smell of
pilchards from father to son.

" You Barbatincas are all born with the smell of
herrings in your hair," the local wags used to say
to Corrado Smelly Head.

" But man is born bald, without any hair, you
thick-headed ignoramuses ! " shouted the salter-
violinist.

One evening at the tavern, not knowing what
to do to shield himself from the sound of that
hateful nickname, he did not hesitate to slam the
door in the face of everybody, shouting : " My
mother was no better than she should have been,
my father was a cuckold, my grandfather was
even more so : I am the son, the grandson of
bastards !   So I am not one of the Smelly
Heads ! "

Naturally, these methods were of no avail.

But when Thou Sufferest had need of him, he
showed himself to be a friend.

Indeed he usually treated Thou Sufferest as such, allowing him to come and dip his daily bread in the strong-smelling salt of the barrels. Now Thou Sufferest was wont to live on bread and on three anchovies a day. For thirty years he had enjoyed an open account at Smelly Head's shop, who gave him credit, but did not fail to keep a record thereof in the black book of debtors. Every now and then the drysalter would say : " You are costing me a fortune ! " And Thou Sufferest, full of embarrassment and of affection, would hang his head and remain silent.

" Three hundred *liras* and forty-two *centimes* ! " grumbled the precise shop-keeper. " But as it is you, I will have patience for another week."

Thou Sufferest felt his heart swelling with awe and with gratitude. He had never even seen three hundred *liras*, all at once.

But his gratitude attained the heroic heights of passion when Corrado, since Thou Sufferest was the only one who did not call him Smelly Head, defended him against the impresario.

This affair was less simple than it may at first appear.

In one thing alone Thou Sufferest stood out against Corrado. Being the son of a servant at the Duke's court, in which capacity he drew from Vienna a microscopic pension of five *liras* a month, his upper lip and chin were clean shaven; he was moreover extremely religious and a musician in the Cathedral chapel, and consequently a doughty reactionary.

Corrado, the son of liberals and the product of his own work, a free-thinker and a demagogue, ostentatiously displayed a red tie and Cavallotti moustaches (1) upon which, since he had the habit of twirling them frequently with his fingers, the brine acted both as wax and as a cosmetic.

Corrado would have liked his friend to repudiate the pension from Vienna, the wages of tyranny. He even offered to take him into his own house, but Thou Sufferest steadily refused. Friends, yes, but out of doors. He would never have entered the house of an unbeliever, who refused to receive the priest even for the Easter benediction.

"Then pay for those anchovies!" bawled the drysalter, with a curse, "since you are battening on the gold of tyrants!"

But Thou Sufferest turned a deaf ear to this.

Something in his upbringing as a servant of the aristocracy rendered him refractory to the idea of middle-class dignity. He had the tenacious petitioning humbleness, the abased but ingenuous and self-assured countenance which defy the harshest refusals and are proper to the fallen.

1. Felice Cavallotti (1842–98) was a well-known radical and republican leader during the Italian *Risorgimento*. He wore long, bushy moustaches. The allusion to 'the Duke's court' refers to the period (before 1860) in which this part of Italy was split up into duchies under Austrian control or influence.

In his sphere he was in fact a man who had come down, just as Smelly Head was a social conqueror in his. They were bound together by humbleness on the one side and by contempt on the other, by mutual affection and by their common love for music.

When at the theatre they were accompanying a ' star ' Gilda, or a Manrico (1) as we in Italy understand him, or the Triumphal March in *Aida*, Smelly Head would scrape away at the four strings like a lion, vieing in his oaths with the quivering demisemiquavers in order to give proof of his admiration in the presence of the Eternal ; while Thou Sufferest would reverse his bow and exclaim with an ecstatic grimace :

" Thanks be unto thee, O Lord, for the writing of such music ! "

He used to reverse his bow in order not to make discord.

It was an invariable rule with him, in difficult passages, to turn the wooden side of his bow to the strings ; because he could not play them, avowed his colleagues ; but *he* maintained that it was because his musical emotions affected his sight.

" Will you go and ' confess ' such lies ? " Corrado would ask him. Thou Sufferest would merely blush.

The fact is that when the communal adminis-

1. Well-known operatic characters. Gilda is the heroine in *Rigoletto*, Manrico the hero of the *Trovatore*. Both these operas are by G. Verdi.

tration changed hands, passing from the moderates, that is to say from the " mallow " party (1), over to the socialists, the impresario of the theatre was also changed. The new man, Bagatti, wished to give the citizens a St. Stephen's day (2) worthy of the new age, and he entered the theatre with great projects.

His watchwords were " Get rid of stale traditions," " Clear away the barnacles," " Break up old cliques," " Make for progress " and " Let us have a Temple of Art."

In the end he left things as they were, or perhaps a little worse.

He vented his spleen on Thou Sufferest, because he wore morning, noon and night a white tie.   He declared he could not tolerate that emblem of Reaction.   He pried into the life of the poor second violin, he spied on him during rehearsals, and seized upon his practice of reversing his bow.   He was a brutal man.

" Ah, you Jesuit," he cried, " is it not enough that you should insult the conscience of the people with that courtier's cravat ? "

" What harm can there be in my tie ? " asked the astounded Thou Sufferest, feeling it in order to see if it had got twisted or undone, while

1. *Il partito della malva* was a disparaging sobriquet for moderatism among Italian socialists and radicals.   The origin of this phrase is to be sought in the use of the mallow as an emollient.

2. The 26th of December, that is to say the day on which the winter opera season usually began in Northern Italy.

Smelly Head absent-mindedly hummed : " Courtiers, thou vile and cursed race " (1).

" Your cravat," shouted the impresario, " tells that it was your mother who earned you that Viennese pension at the court of the tyrant ! "

" My father," corrected the poor violinist, without understanding.

" It was your mother," continued Bagatti, " your mother ! And is it not enough for you to insult the people ? Do you also want their blood, must you also treacherously steal their pay ? Impostor, Don Basilio (2), parasite ! "

" I ? " asked Thou Sufferest, in an astonished and awe-struck whisper.

" Who then, I ? " rejoined Bagatti, sarcastically.

Taking the violin from his hand, he showed the orchestra how Thou Sufferest performed difficult passages.

The orchestra had known this for twenty years, but it had not spoken.

The conductor was sorry for the poor fiddler, but he was young and had to think of his career ; so he remained silent. If he had spoken, he also would have got into trouble for not having noticed that strange species of virtuosity.

The impresario returned the violin to Thou Sufferest with these words :

1. A well-known air from *Rigoletto*.
2. Don Basilio is the music master in Rossini's *Barbiere di Siviglia*. The impresario is alluding to his treachery and venality.

"Get out of here, or I will smash it over your head!"

At the thought of losing the glory, comfort and light of his seat in the orchestra, Thou Sufferest, who to keep his post would have suffered any humiliation, regained his courage. The little blood that he had mounted to his long and horse-like head.

"I," he cried, "I who have accompanied Masini in *Lohengrin*, Madame Patti in the *Barber of Seville*, Tamagno in *Othello* and Madame Pasta in *Falstaff*, must *I* go? I who am a friend of Gianfardini, who say thee and thou to him whenever we meet? Never, never! I will die here first!"

Gianfardini was a local celebrity who after a splendid début had lost his voice, but still remained beneath the porticoes of the town and in the wine vaults one who, if his determination had only equalled his voice, could have eclipsed Borgatti and Tamagno and put the happy memories of Rubini and Gayare to shame.

"Did you accompany them with the 'stick' (1)?" asked the impresario, guffawing.

"With 'the stick' and with 'the hair,'" cried the poor fiddler, in tears. "I love music!"

He had touched a delicate chord. The whole orchestra turned in his favour, and the first to

1. 'The stick' and 'the hair' have been found to correspond in the jargon of English violinists to *il legno* and *la setola*, meaning respectively the wood and the horse-hair of a violin bow.

stand up was Corrado who said that he also belonged to 'the party,' but that politics ought not to enter into this matter, and that if Thou Sufferest had lost his agility he should be tolerated because there still remained to him his sweetness of tone, and that in short the orchestra did not intend to stand any bullying.

The Impresario grew obdurate, the orchestra went on strike and the opera season threatened to collapse. Thou Sufferest became a martyr to his love for music, and no one cared any more whether he knew his art or not. The impresario had to surrender and allow him to come back, offering him half excuses which Thou Sufferest accepted with more embarrassment than they were tendered with.

" I cannot make out what it is that makes me sacrifice myself for you," Corrado kept repeating to him. " I keep you alive with my anchovies and I also compromise my political career." Indeed he persuaded himself, and persuaded his friend, that he had seriously compromised his chances of a seat in the town council by that act of insubordination.

Thou Sufferest's affection then became a passionate devotion. But as a rule he could not express himself in words ; for this he required terrible situations like the one Bagatti had forced upon him.

He remained silent, and Smelly Head concluded with profound contempt : " I have sacrificed myself for an ungrateful man."

"But I tell you . . ." stammered Thou Sufferest.

"Don't tell me anything," replied the dry-salter, looking hard at him, "you had better not ! We democrats only need the testimony of our conscience. *We* do not need auricular confession ! By the way : a fat lot of help your priests have given you ! " For it must be recorded that the clerical party had understood that by bestirring itself it would have done harm to Thou Sufferest, and therefore, being worldly wise, had pretended to take no interest in the affair, watching meanwhile to see what would happen. Rome knows and teaches the value of time. But Thou Sufferest could not understand these subtleties, and his friendship and gratitude were cruelly setting him at variance with his conscience as a good Catholic.

These tribulations, these sacrifices of the spirit, which he could not express, he offered up to friendship as devout women will offer their sorrows unto Christ. He went so far as to pray in church for Corrado Barbatinca, and he thought he would do well to tell him about it, but had to flee with his fingers in his ears as a safeguard against the flood of impieties and taunts with which the diabolical salter inundated his shop and the portico.

Yet at midday he returned for his three anchovies, and Corrado was cruel enough to reproach him for accepting credit from an unbeliever. Obedient to his abject conscience as a parasite, full of perturbations, Thou Sufferest ate the anchovies as a libation to friendship.   He merely said in his humble way :

"The pension from Vienna is no longer enough ; everything is getting dearer.   Alas, what times we live in ! "

A parasite he was, and such he remained.   To ask was for him an impulse both of affection and sympathy.   He asked for little, but he asked for everything, always : for anchovies, for resin to rub on his bow strings, for a score on which to sit in order that he might be a little higher on his seat.

He had very long flabby legs and his body was limp and shrunken, as though he had always just come in out of a shower of rain ; while Corrado, copious and flourishing as a full-blown sunflower, leaned upon Paganini's instrument with a triple chin and a hefty jaw.   "I could break the violin with my chin ! " he boasted.

"My dear fellow," he would cry when at the Musicians' Bar during the intervals, "the art of the violinist has always been under the protection of the Devil.   Think of Paganini, think of Tartini !   Why, come now, of course you also will have to give him your soul ! "

Thou Sufferest would stop his ears, begging nevertheless :

"Will you stand me a glass of liqueur ? "

"If you will repeat with me," answered Smelly Head excitedly : "Our Father which art in Hell, thy kingdom come ! "

Whereupon Thou Sufferest would drown his horror in a glass of *grappa* (1).

" If you won't say it, pay ! " urged the dry-salter. But in the end he used to pay, amidst uproarious laughter.

" Will you give me a caramel ? " This was Thou Sufferest's constant request while he was playing at a performance.

" Won't you give me a caramel ? " At last, Smelly Head ended by making one out of vile hen-droppings.

" Why, it tastes like . . . " mumbled the half-poisoned Thou Sufferest, in the middle of an orchestral *fortissimo*.

" That's just what it is ! " replied his friend, squirming on his seat, " That's just what it is ! "

Now either of them would have been most surprised if any one had asked which was the fonder of the two. Thou Sufferest was unable to express himself, he could not even think, and Corrado regarded himself as nothing less than a paragon of generosity and friendship.

Very soon three things happened.

Thou Sufferest received a small legacy from a relation of whose very existence even he had been ignorant, and was thus enabled to pay for all the anchovies he had eaten during thirty years of friendship ; Smelly Head died one morning of a sudden stroke and without suffering ; and Thou Sufferest was disqualified and dismissed from the theatre.

1. A kind of cognac.

A young conductor had come who was exceedingly able, celebrated and severe, full of the high notions he entertained concerning music and himself : an æsthete, an un-human being, in short. This virtuoso had been asked to conduct the opera season and a few orchestral concerts. Thou Sufferest, accustomed as he was to the kindly faces of the old conductors he had known, trembled in his heart. " Misfortunes never come singly," he thought, " and I have lost Corrado."

The orchestral concerts, full of that frightful symphonic music in which every part is difficult and where every instrument plays an important part, terrified him no less than the Day of Judgment. He looked at the black, swarming pages with the anguish of an illiterate man who has been given his death sentence to read.

It is a common habit with conductors to shout, to stamp and to storm. One knows, however, that they are merely giving vent to their feelings, and that it will all blow over. But this wise youth was cool and self-possessed, and his politeness was such that it positively took one's breath away. As soon as he had tested the orchestra, he turned to the Theatrical Committee, which was expecting the usual compliments, and politely uttered these few words : " One and all disqualified."

When their astonished exclamations had subsided, the discussions, the negotiations, the detailed consideration of each individual case, began; but the conductor would only yield a point with exasperating reluctance. So the Committee, presided over by an old musical enthusiast, resorted to the expedient, which seemed to it advisable, of intimidating the young and peremptory baton ' star ' with the scarecrow of public opinion. The old case of Thou Sufferest was recalled and duly illustrated and coloured, in fact they made of it little less than an orchestral conspiracy and a sedition on the part of the citizens.

The poor last second violin suffered cruelly through all this.

The conductor, who prided himself upon seeing everything and upon knowing even the stems of the notes in each part, wished for nothing better. He assembled the orchestra, announced the piece which was to be tried, and before raising his baton coolly said : " What is the name of the last gentleman in the second violins ? "

" Thou Sufferest," whispered his colleagues, " Thou Sufferest, he wants you."

" Me ? " said Thou Sufferest, awaking from his lethargy.

When the poor violinist had come to his senses and surprise had given way to consternation, the conductor asked him to play his part alone.

It was I don't know which among the most difficult symphonic poems of Strauss. Thou Sufferest, as though in a dream, tried to play it. After all, there was nothing else to be done.

The result was something not easy to describe :

a concert of discords, the wail of a dying cicada, a weird sound as of a carpenter's file.

Impassive and unperturbed, the celebrated young conductor stood waiting for the end, indicating the time every now and then in order that the wretched man might accelerate his pace. Perhaps it was fear or perhaps it was the sense of falling over a precipice, the headlong fury of disaster, which went to the head of the second violin, but at a certain point he began to flourish his bow and give a display of virtuosity. In the orchestra laughter got the better of consternation. Thou Sufferest, turning and twisting like a Polar bear, upset his score on to the floor. It was given back to him, and he buckled to it for a few more bars, then lost himself altogether, put the violin under his arm and rubbed his eyes.

"Why didn't you go on?" asked the conductor.

"I don't know," stammered Thou Sufferest, "my sight grew dim. I was counting the rests."

"Then you were not even aware," remarked the conductor icily, "that you had replaced your part upside down on the stand."

"And now," he added, turning to the crest fallen Committee sitting in the stalls of the dark, empty theatre, "I think that is enough. If this is the darling of the town, I leave it to you gentlemen to pass judgment."

He won hands down. All Thou Sufferest's protests were of no avail, he fell from all hearts, his colleagues accused him of having brought about the ruin of the municipal orchestra, and the very urchins hooted him in the streets.

His walks were always round and about the theatre, " our greatest theatre," as he used to call it, and the shop of his old friend.   But he only survived for a few months.

He died saying : " Only two beings have ever done me any good : Corrado and my violin. Now that I have lost them both I am content to die."

His violin lay in its shabby case with all its strings broken. He had snapped them in desperation the day he was dismissed.

Why are the most desperate passions the most tenacious ?

The art of the novelist is a philosophical one.

From *Bella Italia*.   Casa Editrice Ceschina, Milano, 1928. (By kind permission of the author.)

VANNI

MANFREDO VANNI was born at Sorano, near Grosseto, in 1860. He took his degree at the *Istituto superiore* of Florence in 1884. He then began his career as teacher of Italian Literature in a technical institute at Arezzo.

In 1889 he was appointed Italian Literature master in the *Istituto tecnico* of Milan, and he held this post until 1925, when he retired. He is at present actively engaged in preparing or supervising a number of new editions of Italian classics, which will be published by Carlo Signorelli of Milan.

Vanni's works comprise poems, critical essays, short stories, translations from the French and English classics, and numerous didactic works.

He is best known for his *novelle* or short stories, and more especially for the collection published under the title : *Casi da novelle* (1915). Among his poetical works, we may mention : *Gli ultimi epigrammi* (1897), *Epigrammi vecchi e nuovi* (1915), *Epigrammi inediti* (1921), *Pesciolini d'Arno* (1923). His critical essays include, among other dissertations on Italian art and literature : *Girolamo Gigli nei suoi scritti polemici e satirici* (1888), *Pietro Aldi, pittore* (1888), and *Un bruscello in Maremma* (1905).

THE RULE OF ST. FRANCIS

AS fate would have it, *Sor* (1) Ottorino had only just left Vignone (2), when his horse lost a shoe ; at Ricorsi it grew lame, and at Radicòfani it could no longer walk. In order not to injure the animal, he was compelled to leave it at Radicòfani, to rest and recover. Meanwhile he proceeded on foot, feeling sure, however, that at the Sforzesca Post-house he would find some sort of a mount.

He soon perceived that at a short distance in front of him were walking two Franciscan friars, gravely and collectedly as they are wont to do, with their arms thrust into their wide sleeves, and with those steps of theirs which they seem to be counting one by one. *Sor* Ottorino put his faith in them at once, as in the unexpected good fortune of an excellent company ; and he joyfully hastened his steps : for indeed, with a travelling companion, one does not suffer half as much from the tedium of the road ; and if, being in company, one can keep up a lively conversation, one is hardly aware of the journey at all.

He soon overtook them, and immediately greeted them with :

1. *Sor* is the common Tuscan abbreviation of *Signore*, which corresponds to the English Mr.

2. Vignone, Ricorsi, Radicòfani, and the other places mentioned in this story, are small towns or villages in Central Italy, between Siena and Viterbo.

" Praise be to St. Francis ! "

"And with him may the Lord be ever praised!" answered the friars who, being Franciscans, attached great value to such a greeting. Indeed, after this, you may be sure of making their acquaintance.

" From what monastery ? Where are the Fathers going ? May I travel with you ? . . . Why, certainly ! . . . The pleasure is mine. How long these roads are ! . . . Now, you are from such-and-such a place ! " . . . In short, they were soon old acquaintances.

" It's hard, is it not, this life of a brother of St. Francis ? "

" My Master, when one has chosen it and one is aided by God and St. Francis, why should it be hard ? "

" I understand, Father : one can get used to anything. But at first, it must be hard to accustom oneself ! You have to go about, winter and summer, wrapped up in that sack of thorns. . . . For it is always the same habit, is it not, Father Cesario ? "

" That is the Holy Rule."

" Fancy having to wear a heavy, prickly cloth like that, which would flay me alive if I were to keep it on for a single hour ! Because, it's next to the skin, is it not ? You are not allowed to wear anything under your habit, are you ? "

" That is the Holy Rule."

" And you are obliged to travel always on foot !

Yes, we even have a saying : *On St. Francis's horse* (1). Is it true then that the brethren of your order cannot ever go on horse-back ? "

" That is the Holy Rule, my Master. In his Rule, St. Francis desired that the brethren should be forbidden all superfluities. Thus, we are to eat just enough to keep us alive, to dress sufficiently to cover ourselves, and in all things to practise humility, great humility. We cannot, for example, contradict in any manner; and when in company with others, we are enjoined to follow their wishes : so long, of course, as they be not displeasing to God."

" I understand ; but firstly and always obedience to the Holy Rule ! "

" No, my Master. If you take or receive us into your house and offer us food, the Rule enjoins us to obey our benefactor. If you give us little, we eat little ; if you give us plenty, we endeavour to make the best of your bounty, and not to consider whether your meat be fat or lean, or whether we get roast cockerels or bean salad. We are to accept everything with equal cheer, and to refuse nothing : in order not to offend by an act which might be interpreted as pride, and would certainly not be humility. We must, however, observe the strict Rule in what concerns only ourselves, in what depends entirely upon ourselves, as, for instance, in never carrying money about us." . . .

" Oh, is that so ? You cannot ever carry

1. The Italian equivalent to : *On Shanks's pony.*

money about you ? Why, of course : of what use would it be to you ? "

" Of no use. We must live on charity."

" I see, on charity. But sometimes you must be compelled to do without a good many things."

" Oh, no. God and St. Francis always provide for the poor little brother."

" What you say is all very fine, my Father ; but that such a life be not hard and full of suffering, I do not believe."

" My Master, God and St. Francis will reward us in proportion to the resistance we offer against our weaknesses and desires. Do you not think so ? "

Thus saying, Father Cesario straightened his head and shoulders above his robust body, and flashed through his spectacles certain radiations of a controlled and suppressed vitality which acted as a full and visible commentary to his words.

Meanwhile evening had come ; it was growing dark, and night was upon them. Our travellers had barely time, in the dusk, to find the Paglia Inn.

The host, a certain Torello Scrìccioli, who hailed from Samprugnano, came with a lamp to receive the three new-comers : and with a smile on his lips, for *Sor* Ottorino was an old acquaintance of his, and in those days, either through religion or for the sake of prudence, monks were more respected than they are nowadays, when there is not much religion and still less prudence.

A minute later, in came Giorgetto with a platter, which he placed in view on the table. In its spacious emptiness there lay a diminutive roast cockerel.

" All we have left is this roast cockerel, and a thin stick of bread : to-morrow, you see, is our market day at Acquapendente."

" A miserable roast cockerel for the three of us ! " meditated *Sor* Ottorino, while Torello and Giorgetto were laying the table cloth.

The friars, aside, and almost in the darkness, seemed to be waiting quietly and calmly for what God would send them, whether much or little.

After a short while, *Sor* Ottorino, who had been ill concealing his fear of not being able to appease his hunger that evening, said, stretching forth his legs and gazing intently at the toes of his boots :

" Ah, Father Cesario, what a pity it is that your Rule should forbid you to eat roast cockerels ! With the hunger that I have this evening, that lean cockerel will only just tickle my palate ; but I would willingly have shared it with the two of you. . . . See what comes of binding oneself to *rules* ! As I said a short time ago : it is hard, sometimes, it is really hard, this Holy Rule ! Ah, I would never have become, nor shall I ever think of becoming a brother of St. Francis ! One never knows what may happen. Isn't that so, Father Salvatore ? "

This thrust was intentionally directed towards the sweeter character of the two, who with his wonted resignation, resembling indifference, had begun to nibble and eat almost devoutly ; but it was parried by Father Cesario, who waited a while in silence until the host had left the room and then said in a calm, unruffled voice :

" I see, my Master, that you are joking. But I can assure you that we are content to live according to the spirit of charity we find in those among whom our lot is thrown. See, this supper, for instance, is more than enough for me. The bread is all I want."

And only then did he begin to nibble it, with the listlessness of a boy who has just risen in satiety from the table.

The following morning, when the host went to call them, they were all ready for their journey.

There were no mounts, but they had nothing to carry ; so they were soon out of the inn and on their way to Pitigliano.

Sor Ottorino was still chuckling over what had happened the previous evening ; his merriment shone in his eyes and on his lips. Only, he was disappointed at not perceiving on Father Cesario's countenance the faintest sign of his still remembering the jest which had been carried so far.

They were proceeding on their way, in the early morning, with the fresh step that follows a good night's rest.

"A fine morning !" said *Sor* Ottorino, by way of starting a conversation ; but to no purpose. He then noticed that the two friars, while walking, were quietly murmuring their morning prayers ; so, moved by a kind of respect, he held his tongue and walked on in silence.

"A fine morning, but later on the sun will be rather too hot, with this clear sky !" answered Father Cesario, when they had gone a little farther, thereby indicating that, having said their prayers, the two Franciscans had become again two agreeable travelling companions.

And this was an easy beginning to a conversation on general matters, conducted with mutual courtesy and equanimity. *Sor* Ottorino soon forgot all about the game of give and take which he had so indiscreetly begun the previous evening.

As soon as they were in sight of the Paglia, *Sor* Ottorino asked :

"How full is the Paglia, at this time of the year ? Do you know whether it can be forded easily ? . . . I wonder !"

Before he had time to receive any kind of an answer, he found himself confronted by the river itself, which was swollen and rather turbid owing to recent torrential rains ; so that, like a practical man, he answered his own question :

"H'm ; on a horse, it would be easy enough. But on foot, it will be a pretty business !"

"Yes, my Master, yes, it will be," confirmed

Father Cesario. "If instead of boots, socks, trousers and drawers, you had on only a pair of sandals, like we have . . . There ! " So saying, he took them off ; and Father Salvatore soon did the same. Then, with equal ease, they raised their tunics and . . . well, they had no reason to fear those few inches of running water.

But for *Sor* Ottorino, it was a very different matter ; he looked at his boots, he looked at the water ; he began with many an emphatic shake of the head and ended with repeated, ungainly grimaces, as though he had before him a bitter mouthful and at the same time felt very hungry.

" Well, it *is* a pretty business ! Oh, that horse ! Why *did* it break down like that ? " . . .

Father Salvatore had already stepped quietly into the water, and was wading across, when Father Cesario suddenly abandoned his dignified carriage and, bending down with solicitude to-wards *Sor* Ottorino, said :

" My Master, what do you say ? . . . I have good shoulders, and you can trust yourself to them : mount astride ; all you will have to do is to hold my sandals, and in a few seconds I shall reach the other side."

Sor Ottorino was delighted with the idea.

" Splendid ! Splendid ! Thank you, Father ; you are doing me an excellent service."

Father Cesario presented a beautiful pair of rounded shoulders to *Sor* Ottorino who, throwing his arms round the friar's neck and drawing up first one leg and then the other, finally mounted astride : laughing the while, for it seemed to him a funny business. Father Cesario also laughed, but less heartily, and more from within. While the friar, with a certain calm but rather mocking air, was giving him his sandals to hold, one in each hand, *Sor* Ottorino caught a glimpse of this feline laugh, but it was only later that he understood it fully, when he had occasion to remember it and that most clearly.

Having tucked up his tunic with his hands, as before, Father Cesario stepped into the water and proceeded ; but with a certain slowness, which was not altogether due to circumspection.

" Am I very heavy ? " asked *Sor* Ottorino rather breathlessly, by reason of his not too comfortable posture.

" H'm, you are not a dew-drop, you know. . . . You are fat. I can see that you treat yourself well, and that you are not like me : a poor brother of St. Francis ! "

Father Cesario had already taken three or four steps into the water, and these pointed words were a flea in *Sor* Ottorino's ear. His uneasiness increased when, all at once, he felt the friar stop short, right in the middle of the stream. Then he thought that he understood, that he understood only too well ; but he was immediately reassured by the calm and patient demeanour of the man, and by his equally calm voice.

" These sandals . . . they are a great encumbrance round my neck, and they prevent you from holding on as you should do. . . . See if you can throw them over there, on to the dry land."

Sor Ottorino, breathing freely again, now that he saw what was really the matter, obeyed with a relieved countenance. The friar's heavy sandals resounded on the gravel.

" Come along, Father ! "

" Oh, there is no need to hurry now . . . we have only three or four more yards to go ! See, rather, whether you can arrange yourself better : you weigh like a ton of bricks ! "

Sor Ottorino readily endeavoured to balance himself more lightly ; but Father Cesario, beneath him, did not appear to be any the more comfortable, and panted and turned and twisted, without raising a foot to proceed. When, all at once, he asked :

" But . . . what are you carrying with you that you should weigh so horribly ? I feel like St. Christopher (1), with the world upon his shoulders ! "

" Why, what should I be carrying, Father ? Try and hurry up, for you seem to me to be spell-bound. . . . At least get through this part of the river, where the flood is fullest ! "

" Quite so ; we are in the middle, we are in

1. An allusion to an old legend, according to which St. Christopher is supposed one day to have carried across a raging torrent a child which grew heavier and heavier, until it seemed to him that he had the whole world on his shoulders. The child, on enquiry, made himself known as the Creator and Redeemer of the world. (See *The Catholic Encyclopedia*.)

the heart of the river, and the flood is at its fullest : that is why it is so difficult to move. But, now I think I understand. Tell me : are you by any chance carrying money about you ? "

" Why yes, Father. You will understand that we men of commerce must always carry some about us."

" Alas ! Alas ! " cried the friar in a contrite and doleful voice, " Wretch that I am ! Woe to me that I should be carrying money ! Do you not remember the Holy Rule ? "

" What are you talking about, Father ? Are you going out of your mind ? What has the Holy Rule to do with this ? "

" What has it to do with this ? Then have you forgotten that we brethren of St. Francis cannot on any account carry money about us ? "

Sor Ottorino was perspiring ; but he did not answer.

" My dear Master, the Rule is the Rule. Here we must do one of two things : either you throw away all the money you have about you . . . or I must throw you into the water ! "

" Father Cesario, for charity's sake, for the love of God, for St. Francis." . . .

" Throw away your money ! "

" For charity's sake, my dear Father, stop this jesting. . . . Think what you are doing to a poor Christian." . . .

" The Holy Rule demands it. Will you or will you not throw away your money ? . . .

You do not answer ? . . . Well, I shall throw you into the water ! "

Whereupon, Father Cesario, with the massive strength of his bull-like shoulders, shook off *Sor* Ottorino, who first of all went *plump*, *plash* into the full stream, and after a good ducking appeared half out of the water, like a frog, bellowing in his bewilderment:

" Woe is me ! Woe is me ! Murder ! Murder ! Help ! "

But Father Cesario, with two or three vigorous strides, had already reached the other side, from which Father Salvatore, half amazed and half afraid, had been looking on.

As soon as he touched dry ground, Father Cesario turned round to see whether *Sor* Ottorino was able to stand the current, and since he saw that the latter had now raised himself right out of the water, which only reached above his knees, and heard him ever more loudly and furiously, and therefore ever more unmistakably alive, shouting, imprecating and cursing, he calmly went and picked up his sandals and still more calmly put them on. Then, together with his companion, he proceeded on his way with the quiet, modest steps of a Friar Minor.

From *Casi da Novelle*. (A. Taddei, Ferrara, 1915.)

THE END